The Theory of Assessment

An Introduction

Julie Cotton

KOGAN PAGE

London • Philadelphia

Also in the Learning and Assessment Theory series

The Theory of Learning Julie Cotton
The Theory of Learners Julie Cotton
The Theory of Learning Strategies Julie Cotton

First published in 1995
Reprinted in 2002

Kogan Page Limited
120 Pentonville Road
London N1 9JN

© Julie Cotton, 1995

British Library Cataloguing in Publication Data

A CIP record for this book is available from the British Library.

ISBN 0 7494 1709 9

Typeset by Saxon Graphics Ltd, Derby

Printed and bound in Great Britain by Biddles Ltd
www.biddles.co.uk

Contents

Introduction

This book is for every full-time and part-time teacher, including trainers, further education lecturers, work-based skills trainers, higher education lecturers, adult education lecturers, instructors, professors, open learning managers, tutors, distance learning writers, counsellors, mentors, staff development managers and even, as one of my students called himself, apprentice masters. We are all concerned with helping other people to learn and we all need to manage our own learning.

Assessment is not a bolt-on extra to teaching and training but an integral part of planning, preparation and delivery. Indeed, good assessment is a consolidating tool within the learning process. Well-taught students and well-practised trainees can enjoy assessment because the process will give them a chance to show off their knowledge and skills. Praise and recognition for learning well are rewards for hard study work and examiners should take care to make tests and the issuing of results pleasant occasions. In this book I describe the theory behind many different methods of testing and assessment so that you will be able to choose ways to suit the subject and your learners. Provided that the assessment methods are reliable and valid it might suit your learners to be given the choice at the end of a programme, such as portfolio assessment or final examination.

It is difficult to say where assessment ends and evaluation begins because the same tools can be used for each process. I have taken the generally accepted view that assessment is the process of judging individual learners and evaluation is the process of judging learning programmes, including teacher performance. As always, I aim to help the reader to be autonomous in learning, so the final chapter covers the evaluation of your own performance.

This is an introductory book with suggestions for activities to help you to apply the theory to your work. There are open questions within the text to encourage you to pause and consider the implications of the theory. These are not 'self-assessment questions', but merely an encouragement for you to stop and reflect.

Assessment and evaluation methods are open to wide abuse because many teachers and trainers do not understand the rules and the underpinning theory. This book begins with the nature of knowledge itself so that we have a clear idea of what it is we are trying to assess.

5

Chapter 1

Success in Assessment

 CONCEPTS

Passing and succeeding
The nature of knowledge
Successful practice
Successful thinking
Successful attitudes
Matching the assessor's requirements

PASSING AND SUCCEEDING

What a feeling when you first know that you have got the job. What a boost to your self-image when you gain a Certificate of Competency. How useful the extra money will be when you have successfully completed your training or apprenticeship! Oh, the relief when you see your name on the pass list. Most of us experience the joy and pride of success in assessment even if it is just throwing away the 'L' plates after passing the driving test.

THE NATURE OF KNOWLEDGE

This introduction to assessment will look at the nature of what has been achieved in success – getting the job or certificate of competence, completing training or passing an examination.

There are many factors which are taken into account at a job interview, some may be bizarre. I am convinced that I got my first post in teaching because I wore a wide-brimmed pale blue hat at the interview; I knew that the Chairman of the Governors was the local Conservative Member of Parliament. My success may not have said much about my academic standing or my teaching experience but there was clear proof that I scored well on social skills and interpersonal relations.

Certificates of competence are awarded after a group of assessments. The successful candidate has to show perceptual skills in recognizing what needs to be done and the physical ability to carry out the necessary tasks with dexterity and accuracy. Underlying these performance skills the successful candidate needs to be able to prove knowledge and understanding of the whole range of the skill to ensure mastery of every situation in which the same problem may arise.

Successful training usually covers a wide range of physical, knowledge and social skills but training programmes tend to be less general and concentrate on the specific needs of the organization and the individual. The production worker does not need to show a general ability to use machinery but the ability to use specific machinery on the production floor. The accountant does not need to show general knowledge of accountancy at all levels but the ability to work within the accounts and finance department of a particular business. The receptionist needs to demonstrate social and interpersonal skills according to the organization's specific policy; the health worker has to show personal skills according to the standards laid down in a particular branch of the caring professions. Success in training is showing that you can work to a tailor-made set of conditions.

Success in examinations, whether practical or written, depends on the candidate's ability to demonstrate a grasp of factual knowledge and an understanding of procedures. This area is often called 'knowledge' but it is only one part of knowledge. Assessment covers all aspects of human learning:

Facts	Materials
Principles	Numeracy
Rules	Language
Procedures	Practice
Bodily movement	Design
Social skills	Construction
Problem solving	Literature
Human emotions and responses	Empathy
Values and attitudes	Law
Management	Cooperation

The list of what can be assessed is as wide as human experience itself.

ACTIVITY

What did you know when you succeeded?
Suppose you have just passed the driving test. You know how to change gear, steer, use the car's controls and look in the driving mirror. You know how to think about all the outside information on road conditions, other drivers and the mechanics of your own car and come up with a string of driving decisions to guide your physical actions. In addition to your physical and mental knowledge, you have to know the right attitude to other road users and you value safe practice and respect the laws of the land. Now think about an occasion when you succeeded in assessment and answer the following questions:

- What practical skills did you have to show?
- What thinking did you need to demonstrate?
- How did you show you had the right attitude?

Benjamin Bloom (1964) divided the domains of knowledge into three:

- Psychomotor – the area of practical skills
- Cognitive – the area of thinking and factual knowledge
- Affective – the area of feelings and value judgements.

All assessment in every field of work, education and training includes a part of each of these areas of knowledge. There can be no assessment of a purely physical performance because there is always the thinking element. All actions and thoughts take place within a social and cultural environment which affects attitudes, feelings and values. This is a good time to stop and think about what Bloom means in his knowledge classification.

⇨ **STOP AND REFLECT** ⇦

What is a chef thinking about when he or she selects a knife for a new task in food preparation?

What are the physical skills of a lawyer's job?

Would you change your working habits if you moved to another country or a different organization?

SUCCESSFUL PRACTICE

There are different physical movements which may bring you success during assessment. My friend, Amber, plays viola in a string quartet. The minute, swift and perfect fingering on her instrument brings her appreciation and applause; such delightful music is only achieved by dedic-ated, daily practice and it is similar to the manual dexterity achieved by a surgeon or watchmaker. Bodily movement and grace are an essential part of many jobs where inter-personal skills are important.

I once attended a fascinating, hour-long lesson when a trainer of hotel receptionists taught a group of 15 students how to enter a room, close the door and walk towards a group of seated people. This seemingly artless poise can be learned like any other physical skill; I delight in seeing customers melt under the effect of a well-trained reception-ist. Sometimes the physical skills are judged on the final product. Our plumber Tom has made such a splendid job of the pipework in the roof space at home that the plumbing is a work of art. Few visitors to the house inspect the roof space but when Tom wants more work, all he has to do is put together a few sections of pipe to demonstrate his successful practice. Over the centuries craftsmen and artists have made samples of their work to demonstrate the standard of their skill to potential clients. The modern equivalent of this process is a portfolio of evidence to illustrate competency.

⇨ **STOP AND REFLECT** ⇦

What type of physical movement is being assessed in the examples I have just given?

Given enough practice, can everyone achieve all types of physical skill?

When assessing a skill with a strong physical element, is it important to show evidence of current practice or do all physical skills never fade?

Reflex movements

Only the older parts of the brain are concerned with reflex movements – those where no conscious thinking delays the reaction time. Although people can be trained to adapt their reflexes when learning coping skills for an emergency, many of these movements depend on the physical charac-teristics of the individual.

Individual reflex movements are assessed, but this assessment is usually used before a learner starts a programme which involves accurate, quick-paced move-ment skills. For example, dental technicians have to be able to perform delicate hand movements. The Crawford

Manual Dexterity test is widely used when selecting for dental technician programmes. In this test the student is asked to work small headless screws through a hole in a steel plate using a small screwdriver and then place small steel pins into tiny holes in the plate with a pair of tweezers, followed by a collar on top when the pin is in place.

When successful practice depends on the physiological characteristics of the student or trainee it is a good idea to make sure that individual applicants possess the basic reflexes and reaction times. Many tutors and trainers devise entry skills tests when successful practice is heavily dependent on reflex movements.

Physical fitness

Nowadays few jobs and the associated tests depend on physical power and human size but many still rely on physical fitness for success. Obviously the assessment of physical fitness comes into such occupations as the police, all the caring professions, the armed services and the travel and tourism industry, but minimum standards of fitness are laid down for most occupational areas. Recruits and serving personnel may have to have regular medical tests such as blood pressure, heart rate and tests for eyesight or hearing. Routine care and attention to diet, exercise and physical health will always contribute to successful practice.

Non-discursive movements

These are the body movements which illustrate and accompany verbal communications and expressions of an individual's emotions and personality. I gave the example of the hotel receptionist trainer teaching the students how to walk into a room. Bodily communication and facial expression are conditioned by human emotional reaction and social learning, but they can be trained and changed. Instinctively most people believe non-verbal communication rather than the spoken word, so bodily movement, facial expressions and tone of voice are important in successful practice.

Skilled movements

These are produced by bringing together all aspects of knowledge: procedural knowledge, perception and bodily movements combine to make a skilled performance. The assessment of skilled movements is the basis of all training assessment and all National Vocational Qualifications in England and Wales (see pages 110 and 121). Competency-based assessment is the observation of performance together with questioning to make sure that underpinning knowledge is understood. The most usual assessment tools are the checklist and verbal questioning.

The guidelines for successful practical skills are built on job analysis and the accepted standards for the trade or profession. Normally we think of physical skills as a forward progression of improvements on existing practice but this is not always the case. When Upark, the eighteenth century house on the Sussex Downs was destroyed by fire it was painstakingly restored to its condition the day before the fire. There were problems in aging materials to match the condition of rescued scraps of decoration and woodwork but the greatest difficulty was training modern craftsmen and women to achieve the old, lost skills of carving, plastering and decorating. The standards and performance criteria for success in skilled performance are fixed by current practice in the field.

Sometimes knowledge of physical skills and practical procedures are less valued than thinking knowledge. Ryle (1949) challenged the 'Descartes' myth' that there is a polar opposition between body and mind: he challenged the idea that our bodies are public and have a mechanical space which is connected with other bodies but our minds are private and take no space at all. Ryle claimed that this separation of the physical and the mental was a myth and causes errors in thinking about knowledge by making our minds like a 'Ghost in the machine'. Gilbert Ryle makes a distinction between:

- 'knowing that' – propositional knowledge of facts and figures which we use for thinking

- 'knowing how' – the procedural knowledge we use to carry out tasks and solve problems.

'Theorists have been so preoccupied with. . . investigating the nature, source, and the credentials of the theories. . . that they have. . . ignored the question. . . how to perform tasks'.

Ryle's argument is raging today. Some academic institutions concentrate exclusively on theoretical study at the expense of practical and procedural knowledge. Descartes' admiration for scientific method can be seen as the one of the roots of the traditional valuing of theory rather than practice; academic study is valued more highly than merely being able to do the job. There seems to be a basic – and to me unacceptable – idea that if you know the theory then the practice can be assumed, but when you demonstrate successful practice no underpinning theoretical knowledge can be assumed.

There is no trace of the second-rate when Ryle describes people who 'know how':

> Their performances come up to certain standards or satisfy certain criteria. But this is not enough. The well-regulated clock keeps good time and the well-drilled circus seal performs its tricks flawlessly yet we do not call them 'intelligent'. We reserve this title for the persons responsible for their performances. To be intelligent is not merely to satisfy criteria but to apply them, to regulate one's actions and not merely to be well-regulated. A person's performance is described as careful or skilful if in his operations he is ready to detect and correct lapses, to repeat and improve on successes, to profit from the examples of others. . . an action exhibits intelligence, if, and only if, the agent is thinking what he is doing. . .

⇨ **STOP AND REFLECT** ⇦

Do you think that if you know the theory you can carry out the practical task?

Are people capable of achieving high skill levels without understanding underpinning theory?

Should there be a divide between body and mind or are the two interdependent in all human actions?

SUCCESSFUL THINKING

'Knowing that' is usually tested and assessed by asking the learner written or oral questions. This type of knowledge is called 'propositional knowledge' because it represents the best facts, laws and examples that are known at the present time. My mother and I used to laugh at her college notes from the 1920s because they clearly stated: 'There are three vitamins A,B and C'. This was much less to learn than my 1950 notes which covered the B complex, a group of fat-soluble vitamins, and B12 which wasn't discovered until the late 1930s. Like the difference between my mother's knowledge of vitamins and my own, propositional knowledge changes with advances in experiment and proof and this change affects the way in which such knowledge is assessed. I will look at this assessment problem in traditional testing in Chapter 2.

In his book *Assessing Students: How shall we know them?*, Derek Rowntree (1989) makes 17 recommendations which, according to one critic, 'might well be inscribed on tablets of stone for the consideration of all examining boards and assessors'. I have incorporated all his ideas into this introduction to assessment at stages when a simple explanation seems useful. The first Rowntree recommendation emphasizes the importance of overall clarity:

- make certain there are clear aims and objectives
- select the qualities expected from the learner
- make certain you know what the assessment is testing.

I find that Bloom's *Taxonomy of Educational Objectives* (1964) is a useful framework when I am working out which questions to ask to test a candidate's thinking and grasp of theory. There are different levels of thinking, from a quick recall of factual information, which Bloom called 'knowledge' in his classification, to an overall mastery of the whole topic which he called 'evaluation'. This classification dividdes the depth of study into steps of increasing complexity of thought and I have given examples of questions which might be used to test and assess at the each level.

Knowledge – assessing a grasp of simple facts
Assessment is by closed questions because there is always a definite answer at this level. Questions begin with 'Who', 'Where', 'What' and so on and they can be written or oral questions: Who is the Prime minister? Where is the River Nile? What is the square root of four?

These factual questions can be asked in their thousands in multiple-choice questioning and very boring they are! Learners who are quite knowledgeable and who have a good grasp of the subject may get these questions wrong because they cannot be bothered to pay attention, but those who have a fear of failure love to answer this type of question because it is comforting to be proved right. Although confidence may be boosted by the activity, little is learned from such repetitive answering. However, these questions can be used for other purposes such as catching attention when a student is beginning to wander off into a little day-dreaming.

Comprehension – understanding the significance of simple facts and linking basic facts together
Assessment at this stage also uses closed questions to check that the learner knows the meaning of words and has an understanding of simple principles: What is a protein? Why does this engine need a carburettor? When do you use a test of significance? Further questioning can be added as 'probing questions' which can be used to tease out the links between facts. The Socratic tutorial style, in which the answer to one question leads naturally to the next question, is very helpful in testing comprehension. Often the learner does not realize the links between separate pieces of information; by a process of answering linked questions, the learner can be helped to connect and draw together factual knowledge in the working memory.

Application – knowing how to apply facts to the practical situation
This is a useful area of assessment because, like the process of questioning in comprehension, assessment can be used to draw together links in the learner's mind. This time the

links are between 'knowing that' and 'knowing how'; questioning can link the facts stored in the long-term memory with 'how to do things' information.

Assessment can be in the form of strings of questions but it is usually more effective to make the learner work out the order in which application of knowledge should be carried out. We will see in Chapter 4 that objective item testing can be useful in this area, but many assessors use simple practical work to assess.

Any situation where calculations have to be carried out or facts have to be applied can be used: Given the values of the resistances shown in this circuit and a current of two amps, what is the voltage? Calculate the percentage of daily requirement of iron that this pregnant woman would receive from 100 grams of spinach? Calculate the standard deviation of the following raw scores.

Analysis – knowledge gained from the ability to breakdown the whole into component parts
At this level the assessor has to move away from the testing of factual knowledge to the use of questioning to link information and procedures in the learner's mind. Analysis is the technique of breaking processes and problems into their component parts. Learners must be able to demonstrate their ability to identify the building blocks of knowledge.

Suitable testing techniques are those which demand classification and identification; in objective testing (see Chapter 4) multiple response and matching blocks are useful objective testing items and all sorts of structured questions can be used. Practical work and case study analysis are good methods for assessing analysis and the essay or open–book examination can be worded to ask the student to adopt an analytic approach.

The type of question which is asked usually includes the word analyse or analysis: Read the following set of accounts and analyse the profitability of the company. In this case study the manager made several decisions; make an analysis of his management style. How would you test this sample of ore?

Synthesis – knowledge of how to assemble an idea and facts to create a complete final product
Synthesis is the natural counterpart to analysis, so all the assessment techniques which are useful for analysis can be used by the assessor to test the ability to synthesize. This area of knowledge requires the learner to build a theory and assemble a set of given facts, data or resources. The questions might be: How would you plan to develop this site if you were given the following resources? How would you develop a nursing programme for this client?

Evaluation – knowledge of how to assess and evaluate all the other knowledge described in the cognitive domain
Any attempt to assess evaluation skills must use an 'open-ended' method because learners must not be limited by the teacher's or trainer's own grasp of the subject. This does not mean that assessors should not write a marking plan for any assignment set but they should be prepared to adjust such a plan if learners come up with an original angle or unpredicted area in answer to the set question. All project, research, open essay, open book, syndicate method, brainstorming and synectic methods can be used for assessment.

SUCCESSFUL ATTITUDES

In teaching and training we have firm ideas of what a skilled practitioner ought to do, which stretches far beyond cognitive knowledge and skills. We expect learners to have the right attitude, to care and to be responsible. At any stage of assessment, standard psychological testing of personality and attitudes may be used. Bloom joined with his co-workers to suggest several knowledge steps in the affective domain. Again I find these stages which reflect an increasing commitment to professional values and attitudes very helpful when selecting assessment methods.

Receiving or attending – a passive early stage in learning professional attitudes

At this stage of learning young students pay attention only to what is being said and carry out only what they are told to do. There is no real commitment except a willingness to attend. The assessment at this stage is not summative but formative and assessors will be looking for good reports from other teachers, mentors, peers or the learner at this stage. There are several assessment tools available, from formal reports, questionnaires, student feedback forms or personal records to diaries of study and experience.

Responding – the first signs of interest and attention
As learners begin to learn more they become emotionally committed to their work. They comply with and applaud the work and the tasks being undertaken. This should be observed by the assessor in the various ways of collecting evidence mentioned in 'Receiving and attending', above. Most of the assessment tools for this stage are by report and observation because learners are not usually able to formulate and express their own attitudes and feelings.

Valuing – the beginning of commitment
At this stage learners start to take sides and defend the work they are undertaking. Any parent of young students will recognize when their young start to argue strongly in favour of the work and the area in which they are study-ing. The assessor will be able to pick up this development in the affective domain by observation of practice in the psychomotor assessment and the written or verbal responses for cognitive domain assessment.

Organization – the process of personal commitment
It is at this stage of emotional involvement with the work that learners start to rationalize and judge their work by professional standards. They become knowledgeable, are able to discuss any issues which may arise and weigh up the strengths and weaknesses of given examples.

This area of assessment can be added to formal and informal testing and reports on practical performance. Typically, questions on the development of professional attitudes are included in observation checklists and looked for in professional diaries.

Characterization – professional commitment is internalized and becomes part of the individual's personality
This is the stage of professional development at which the work becomes a characteristic of the individual. Personality and psychological tests may be used. The learners have come to believe in their work and the profession is now part of their own self-image and self-esteem. Assessment in this area is the job of those in charge of continuing professional development. The assessment will vary between professional bodies, but personal observation and general conduct at work form the basis of judgement in this area and it has a strong element of peer assessment.

ACTIVITY

Assessing attitudes.
Many trainers and teachers do not recognize the teaching of attitudes as part of instruction, let alone deliberately plan to assess them! Work out which attitudes you think are important and then think about how you assess attitudes in your work.

MATCHING THE ASSESSOR'S REQUIREMENTS

There are many reasons why assessment is carried out (they will be developed in later chapters) but there are two areas of assessment where success depends on knowing exactly what is required. The assessors may have to decide:

- Should the candidate be selected?
- Is this candidate fit to practise?

Anyone who has achieved an offer of employment at the end of a job selection process knows the importance of meeting the assessor's requirements. Hard work and careful research is needed to work out exactly what is required. Assessment as selection has all the difficulties of a competitive situation. When one person is declared the winner, all the rest are losers. In education and training, tough assessment for selection can cause great personal harm to all the learners who have failed. I am not at all sure that some educational establishments would be able to justify their old selection procedures today. When I was a student it was quite common for universities to fail students in their second or third year of studies so that you could have a learner at a very advanced stage of knowledge with no qualification or recognition of earlier study. Nowadays schemes for the accreditation of prior learning and credit accumulation ensure that those who have not been selected to proceed with a course of training or education can utilize their achievement from partially completed learning programmes.

'Fit to practice' assessments are designed to protect the general public from bad practioners. It is assessment to determine whether a learner is likely to maintain high professional standards or to harm whose who are treated by or come into contact with the learner.

I have always been prepared to tell a trainee lecturer or teacher that he or she was a bad performer rather than run the risk of allowing any wretched students to suffer at a bad lecturer's hands. 'You are a rotten teacher; find some other way of earning a living' – no matter how diplomatically phrased – is not the best way to build a trainee teacher's confidence, but as an assessment it does protect the future generation of learners.

There comes a point in such an assessment when the assessor must make a clear decision about the candidate's future practice. As a member of the general public you do not want your pharmacist to get your prescription right 85 per cent of the time; you probably feel that he or she should get the prescription right 100 per cent of the time.

Recent educational theory has pointed out that recognizing the importance of the individual and student-centred learning are major contributions to effective learning theory, but assessment has also to judge quality and standards in some vital areas. 'Fit to practice' assessment has to give firm judgements on what is and what is not acceptable professional procedure.

Chapter 2

Traditional Methods

 CONCEPTS

Measuring existing knowledge
Forms of knowledge
Formative, summative and ipsative assessment
Norm-referenced testing
Methods of formal assessment
Value judgements

MEASURING EXISTING KNOWLEDGE

When I was a girl my Father used to read aloud on Saturday evenings. He started with *Three Men in a Boat* and *Rodney Stone*, moved steadily through the classics with Jane Austen and Dickens before ending, in my early teens, with modern novels which my Mother got from the library. It was a magical time and sometimes we were all so keen that the reading would extend to Saturday night and begin again straight after lunch on Sunday. There is so much to learn when you are young and there is nothing like reading aloud for turning youngsters into voracious readers.

I remember a time when my boys were young and we carried out experiments at home: making butter in the kitchen mixer or looking for indicator plants in the stream.

We had splendid expeditions to see their first sculpture in the Tate and their first proper picture in the National Gallery.

As an adult it is very easy to forget the enormous task for a young person when faced with the depth and width of existing knowledge. Before anyone can learn to be creative or critical there is a great body of language, literature and thinking to be taken into the personal computer – the brain. Traditional methods of assessment measure how far an individual person has progressed in assimilating existing knowledge.

FORMS OF KNOWLEDGE

The nature and content of existing knowledge moves on. Just before I entered the University of London, Crick and Watson made great advances in the field of DNA and genetics. Two years after their major breakthrough in research, my lecturers did not appreciate the significance of their work so I graduated from the university with no knowledge of the new theories. Subsequently I had to carry out a great deal of study before I could teach biochemistry at technical college level. All assessment in biochemistry at this time was affected by the significant change in existing knowledge.

The work of Paul Hirst (1970) is a useful guide for an assessor who has to choose appropriate methods of assessment and questions in different forms of knowledge. Mathematical proof is not suitable for questions of religion and scientific evidence has no place in the judgements of creative arts. Paul Hirst put forward the idea that there were different forms of knowledge with different methods of proof; here is a simple outline of his theory. Once you understand the basic nature of knowledge it is easier to pick questions which test and assess understanding.

Form of knowledge	Proof
Mathematics	Formal logic, axiomatic, self-evident, true by definition eg, the relationship between the diameter and circumference of a circle never varies. All proof is within the subject itself.

Physical sciences	Scientific method. Observation, hypothesis, theories which are progressively tested, corrected, communicated and end in generally accepted results.
Human sciences	Qualified scientific method, because living things are so complex that factor analysis has to be carried out before inferential statistics can be gathered. In addition, human behaviour is unpredictable because people are not always rational or logical.
Fine arts	Proof of beauty and creativity is not metaphysical as so much craft and skill goes into the production of a work of art. The laws of perspective, design, colour theory, sound, touch, language and literature apply to judgements and evaluation of all the arts.
Religion	The ultimate proof of religion is faith, but like the arts there are more than metaphysical questions to be answered. When judging religious knowledge, every religion has a vast language and literature which can be tested as proof of knowledge in this field.
Philosophy	This is a form which is largely a question of metaphysical reasoning. However, even in this tradition, knowledge can be tested by finding out a person's level of familiarity with the language and literature of philosophical argument.

There are shifts in the lores of any subject so that the propositional knowledge in these fields will advance as more human experience and thought is added to the 'literature' of the form of knowledge. When so-called factual knowledge is tested it must be remembered that facts can change.

FORMATIVE, SUMMATIVE AND IPSATIVE ASSESSMENT

There is a common distinction made between assessment which is made during a programme and which is usually aimed at improving learning, and assessment which is used to predict, select or reward learners. Formative assessment methods are designed to establish what progress a student is making during learning and to give feedback on it. Summative assessment methods are designed to establish what a student has achieved at the beginning or the end of a unit, programme or course so that a final mark or grade can be awarded. These summative assessment results can be used in the evaluation of learning programmes, the learning environment or teacher performance. There is a special type of summative assessment which is called 'ipsative'. It measures the progress an individual learner has made as a result of undergoing a learning experience.

Examples of formative assessment

- Assessment at the end of a particular learning session within a wider programme is intended to *establish how much has been learned*. Typically there are verbal questions which are often repeated at the beginning of the next session to help recall. Sometimes a quick written test can be helpful as a summary and a trigger to memory.
- Assessment to *establish progress* is essential for the learner. Testing helps the learner to rehearse, remember and reorganize new material. Be adventurous in the choice of questions so that you can establish new memory links for the learner.

- Assessment also provides *feedback* for the learner which is so essential especially in learning practical skills. Always give the learner as much feedback as possible by relating assessments to subsequent teaching.
- Assessment can *diagnose individual strengths and weaknesses*. Find out if anyone is falling behind so that you can press the panic button and provide remedial learning while there is still a chance of helping the individual to catch up. Wild ducks breed in our creek at home and I feel like the mother duck sometimes when I teach: I constantly round up all my learners to make sure that no one is going astray.

═══════════════ **ACTIVITY** ═══════════════

Helping an individual to catch up.
Teachers and trainers may not have enough time to spend with one individual who has dropped behind. It may be difficult to provide suitable open material for an individual but it is possible to create a quick self-assessment pack by using the information mapping technique in a library or resources centre. Identify a learner who needs remedial study and then write a list of questions which will guide a learner through the main points of the topic in simple steps.

Certificates and other paper qualifications act as a clear focus for learning and as a powerful extrinsic *motivator*. Interim assessment which demonstrates that a learner is on course for the prized success is a strong reason for formative assessment. I am never sure that learners are totally honest in acknowledging the real reason why they put effort into study. Many learners say that they studied hard to pass the examination yet after the event they seem to remember a great deal of personal pleasure and internal satisfaction from the learning experience.

$\Rightarrow$ **STOP AND REFLECT** $\Leftarrow$

Do you think that regular assessment encouraged or discouraged your progress during formal study?

Did you find that the feedback from assessment helped or hindered your learning?

Did you find that you were able to catch up if gaps in your understanding were identified in routine testing?

Assessment also acts as regular *feedback for the instructor or teacher*. Formative assessment can give immediate feedback on the effectiveness of your teaching. When the learners have difficulty in answering questions during a learning session this highlights a point where greater effort should be made the next time the topic is taught. It is also the best point for effective questioning in recap and recall. After a session I mark where students have found questions difficult so that I can practise better explanations.

Examples of summative assessment

Summative assessment occurs at the *end of a programme* and encompasses all written, practical and oral examinations. This *includes phase tests* and all continuous assessment if it is marked at deadlines throughout a learning programme.

Assessment which is carried out to *predict performance or act as a tool for selection* is also of the summative type because the candidate does not have a second chance to resit the test. Assessment can be used for the allocation of places in training and education as well as for employment opportunities, all of which are economically important to the individual applicant. If the training is expensive and there is only enough money for, say, 12 new trainee pilots this year, then the top 12 will be selected and the rest will be failed no matter how good they are. There is little satisfaction or benefit in being rejected even in a good year because the opportunity to benefit from the training is lost.

Assessment can be used to predict a learners's likely performance level in the future. However, some people only have to be told that they are unlikely to do well for the prediction to become a challenge to succeed against every obstacle. Assessment as a prediction is usually better used as a guide rather than a ban.

$\Rightarrow$ **STOP AND REFLECT** $\Leftarrow$

Did you regard predictions at school or college as a challenge or guidance?

Do you avoid giving advice to learners and, if so, why?

Do you sometimes refrain from discouraging a student from a proposed course of study because you are frightened that you might be accused of being ageist, sexist or racist?

Ipsative assessment

Ipsative assessment *measures individual improvement* by comparing the grade or level at the start and the finish of a learning programme. Nowadays funding for training and education can depend on institutional evaluation. For many years some schools and colleges have been careful to select only the brighter students for entry to public examinations so that the overall pass levels appear to be better than other institutions. With the use of computers for record keeping it is quite possible for schools and colleges to be evaluated on the improvement of individual grades and unit achievement of all students. I think that this would be a much fairer assessment of the value of teaching, training and learning.

NORM-REFERENCED TESTING

This assessment system is the basis of traditional methods of assessment in which students are compared to each other and placed in rank order or on a normal distribution curve (see Chapter 5 on statistics). Before any examination is set, the awarding body decides the distribution of grades and sets the pass mark. These decisions are arbitrary and high or low pass percentages can be set which are not dependent on percentage scores in the examination. In any one year each student competes directly with other students sitting the examination at that particular time. The examiners can make comparisons with earlier years and 'jack up' or lower the distribution curve if they feel there has been a general improvement or a fall in overall standards. It is not possible to make a direct comparison of percentage scores on examinations because this year's paper is not the same paper as last year's.

There is one fundamental difficulty about norm-referenced testing and this is the need to spread the students' marks so that a clear rank order can be established. Serious statistical problems of reliability arise if students' scores bunch too closely together, because the differences in grades may depend on only a handful of real marks on an examination paper. In any one subject area the knowledge and practice can be divided into what the student:

must know
should know
could know.

If the essential knowledge (the 'must know') within a subject area is questioned, then most students ought to score well on such questions. The same is true of knowledge which the student 'should know', and it is only in the area of 'could know' that there will be a real stringing out of the students into rank order. This feature of norm-referenced assessment means that there is pressure to ask trivial questions on topics which are peripheral to the subject.

Norm-referenced testing is different from criterion-referenced testing (described in the next chapter) which is a system of comparing each individual's performance against set criteria and standards. The criteria need not be restricted to minimum thresholds of competent, acceptable or safe performance because they can represent mastery and excellence. There is no competition with other candidates in criterion-referenced assessment because, in theory, all students could fail to meet the standards set or all could achieve competence.

METHODS OF FORMAL ASSESSMENT

Written tests and examinations

There is a range of written examinations for the assessor, between highly-structured tests which can be marked by computer and open examinations which rely heavily on the judgement of individual markers.

Objective testing

The construction of objective tests has a great deal in common with all standard testing and the method is covered in Chapter 4. Computer marking is discussed on page 136.

Structured questions

Many modern examinations are carefully laid out with spaces for the student to write answers and a marking tally on the right hand side of the examination paper to inform the student about the weighting of marks for each section. This format reduces variations between markers.

Data input examinations

These are increasingly used in professional examinations. The candidates are given information to study, sometimes some days before the examination and sometimes with a set reading time before the start of the examination. The data may be highly technical, like a full set of financial accounts. Marking schemes are restricted because of the specific nature of the information which has been given.

Open book

The skill tested in this form of examination is the ability to *use* the book concerned and not to *remember* it. In my navigation courses I do not expect my students to remember the tide tables for each day; I expect them to use tide tables for a set problem. Again, like data input examinations, the marking plan is straightforward.

Essay examinations

The questions do not attempt to be a coverage of the syllabus but act as a vehicle for the candidate to display knowledge and discussion at an appropriate level. Markers have to be trained to avoid bias and strong moderation systems are needed to ensure fairness.

There is no reason why marking schemes should be kept secret from the candidate: even when the essay form is used a candidate should learn from previous examiners' reports what is expected in the examination. Research has shown that a lone marker or assessor can place his or her students into rank order, but it is when marks from a group of assessors are combined that the results become unreliable assessment, see page 72.

Do not forget that feedback from written examinations is just as important as feedback in a learning session. There is no reason why a teacher or trainer should not use a standard feedback form when returning student work, rather than scribbling in the margins.

ACTIVITY

A feedback form for the student.
The next time you set an 'end' test paper, write it in the form of a structured paper with a clear marking scheme and write a student feedback form. Check to make sure that the learners get better feedback from this experiment.

Continuous assessment

Continuous assessment seems to involve both students and teachers in a great deal of work. Whereas formal examinations are usually marked with a degree of secrecy, continuous assessment involves the feedback of marked work to the learner with direct face-to-face contact. It is good for the student to have clear feedback but the handing back of work can cause confrontational situations.

Here is a scale of marks which I invented to try to persuade my colleagues to use a fuller scale in a large continuous assessment system:

10 Outstanding
   Some markers never give 10 because they say 'nothing is perfect'. Please pretend that 11 is perfect because if 10 is never used, the scale is reduced to 90 per cent.

9 Excellent
   Use a 9 if you want to give your student a real pat on the back but I would ask those of you who think all of your geese are swans to please use a 9 sparingly.

8 Above average
   About 20 per cent of your students should achieve this level in assignments. Remember that we have stiff entry requirements and students can expect to pass and pass well if they do the work.

7 Average
   It is surprising that about 40 per cent of your students should receive a 7 out of 10. Do not forget that you have to hand this work back 'face-to-face'.

6 Below average
   This is a mark which ought to be given to roughly 20 per cent of your students and it is important that you give a lot of comments for improving the quality of work. Point out where they may apply more theory to practice or make sure that they are giving enough practical examples of the theory.

5 Pass
   This mark should be a warning that the work is very marginal. Make sure that the student does not have fundamental learning difficulties. The 5 grade should warn the student that a major effort for improvement is needed.

4   Marginal fail
        This is a grade to give to a student who is deliber-
        ately not doing enough work, but do be careful
        because such students may have real learning diffi-
        culties and you may need help in finding learning
        support. Do not leave a student at this point; we
        would much rather rescue learners during the course
        than fail them in the final examination.

0 – 3   Fail
        Face-to-face in a small tutorial room you cannot use
        these grades when returning assignments to mature
        students. Remember that we are training teachers
        and we have a responsibility to the learners that our
        students will teach. You may have to advise trainee
        teachers who return such inadequate assignments
        that they have not chosen the right profession! If you
        think that this is a temporary mistake, ask the
        student to repeat the assignment.

When I was offering this advice the same markers were
happy to use 4 as average when marking individual examination questions but the average was 7 when they had to
hand back work face-to-face!

Practical examinations

Often the organization of practical examinations brings out
the best in all staff, who combine to make sure that the
event is a model of cooperation and fairness. Sometimes
the examiners do not give the staff a chance: I will never
forget my second year at university when I went into the
physiology exam and the written instruction was, 'Swallow
the Ryle tube and pump out the contents of your resting
stomach'. Only a few of us survived that examination
which was regarded by the laboratory staff as a joke. There
are so many factors which affect practical examinations that
technical staff need to make certain that all candidates start
from the same advantages and constraints.

Marking schemes for practical work should be clearly
divided into process and product. The marking team will

have to be trained in the use of checklists for performance observation of processes. The team may need to be trained in perceptual skills so that judgements of the quality of final products can be standardized. It is possible to bring up a team of assessors to a fine degree of agreement on quality standards. Fine discrimination and close observation can be learned.

Projects

Control of assessment for project work usually comes down to judgements about the learner's presentation methods and skills. When a student is writing on paper in an examination and fighting to get down enough to pass within a deadline, the presentation of work is not an important factor. Continuous assessment demands better presentation skills, but in projects and portfolio examinations the presentation is of great importance.

$\Rightarrow$ **STOP AND REFLECT** $\Leftarrow$

How much time do you think your project students should spend learning desk-top publishing skills?

How do you arrange for support for the verbal and visual presentations of project work for assessors?

How do you award marks in your marking scheme for such factors as interpersonal skills in the presentation of projects?

Oral examinations

No quality control can be applied to a report of an oral examination if the assessor just says he or she was a good chap or chappess. There must be some form of detailed record of oral examinations if the marker is to be moderated. It is possible to record or video assess sessions but this is very time-consuming. I have found the best way of recording oral examinations is to sit beside a laptop computer and use the screen as a sketchpad for noting down the sequence of questions and answers. It is easy to give a printout to the learner and the internal verifier, and keep a copy for your own records.

Take-away papers

Provided that a candidate has not persuaded a brighter student to sit the examination in their place, formal examinations guarantee authenticity. Project work and continuous assessment may be open to outside help, but good tutorial contact usually makes it possible for assessors to detect this. Take-away examination papers are a different case because the assessor may not have enough personal knowledge of the learner to be able to recognize authentic work from a particular student.

A handwriting test is no use these days; a colleague's son, required to write his exam assignments in his own hand, programmed his computer to write in his handwriting and continued to produce his schoolwork by wordprocessing! Given the continuing developments in information technology it is increasingly difficult for markers to assess the reliability of these examinations.

Portfolios

Many areas of learning lend themselves to the development of a portfolio of selected samples of work and this method is widely used in competency-based learning. It helps the consolidation of learning when a student collects assessment reports with comments from his or her peers, teachers and also examples of self-assessment. Assessment in this case can become an event at the end of a programme or semester. An exhibition of work, presentation, competition or even an open day can become a focal point for the students. Portfolio presentation can be exciting, stressful or a social occasion to round-off successful learning. It is helpful to train the learners in critical skills by allowing them scope for controlled criticism of each others' work, and the presentation of assignments is good practice for interpersonal skills training.

VALUE JUDGEMENTS

All markers are making value judgements whether it is an assessment of theoretical knowledge or the mastery of psychomotor skills. Not even objective item testing marked by computer is free from assessor decisions because the judgement in this type of assessment takes place in the design of test specifications and the writing and selection of items. One of the most difficult biases in value judgement to correct is the individual or group who think that they have a special vision of truth. These may be people who hold strong political or religious views and their judgement can be subconsciously impaired. Students seem to learn very quickly which line to take with particular lecturers if they want to get good assignment marks, but some poor learners are the unwitting victims of markers who are ardent feminists or fundamental religious zealots.

Some markers have to be dropped from the assessment teams because they are unable to show sound value judgements. They may not be able to overcome unconscious bias or they may be lazy and fail to carry out the work conscientiously. Here are some examples of poor marking.

When I was running an examination and continuous assessment team I had a colleague who appeared to be making rogue decisions. I noticed that her marginal and failed students were all very pretty girls. I never proved this bizarre theory but the chief external examiner took my hypothesis sufficiently seriously to ask me to attach a photograph of the student to each of the suspect files of work! In the same system, I had trouble from the engineering section which seemed to think that all engineering students were worth 100 per cent all the time.

A common bias creeps in when some markers reduce scores for spelling and grammatical errors when others do not. The assessor team leader must iron out these individual variations.

I came across a very odd case of unconscious bias one summer. Many formal examinations take place in hot summer months and students do sweat during examinations; I found that I could smell curry or peanut oil as I turned the pages of some scripts! This was distasteful to some of my markers and I found that some had marked down unconsciously.

I caught out one idle fellow by making a genuine mistake. I gave him five scripts to mark twice in the double-marking system. First time he returned the following sequence of marks: 8, 3, 5, 4 and 7, but the second time I got 6, 5, 4, 6 and 9. I suspect he plucked marks out of the air, which is in line with the apocryphal story of grading theses by throwing each one down a flight of stairs. The ones which went the furthest got the highest grades.

Chapter 3

Competency-based Learning

THE BALANCE BETWEEN THEORETICAL KNOWLEDGE AND PRACTICE

'What do you do with a BSc NUT? Oh, what do you do with a degree in nutrition?' This is the refrain of a little number that I wrote for a Christmas review a year before I graduated in nutrition from the University of London. The song went down very well because there were plenty of jokes to be made on the theme, but it did relate to a serious problem. Although we were stuffed to the brim with theoretical and factual knowledge, final-year students had to face the job market and answer the question, 'Yes – but what can you do?' John Yudkin, our professor in nutrition, had similar problems with the university authorities: he had started the new degree some four years earlier and here is a quote from his obituary in the *Daily Telegraph*, Wednesday, 19 July 1995:

> Yudkin had originally proposed a nutrition degree made up of chemistry, biochemistry, physiology and microbiology, including a short course of cookery. This was rejected by the university on the grounds that cooking was not an academic subject. He promptly changed the title to 'food preparation' and the course was accepted.

Competency-based learning comes under heavy criticism from the traditional educationalist but at least potential employers have a clear description of what the applicant is able to do.

There is a view that learning to be competent can be achieved with only a superficial grasp of theoretical principles. I do not hold this opinion; it is impossible to carry out successful practice without a sure grasp of fundamentals. However, some assessors in competency-based learning are obsessed with observing performance and fail to question candidates about their underpinning knowledge. Competency is proved by presenting evidence of skill and knowledge; if the best way to prove underpinning knowledge of higher levels of competency is by sitting a three-hour, traditional examination then there is nothing in the 'rules' of competency-based assessment to say that this assessment tool should not be used. Assessors should pick the best assessment format for the job. On page 134 advances in higher level NVQ assessment are discussed.

⇨   STOP AND REFLECT   ⇦

Consider the balance between theory and practice in your own learning programme.

How did you learn to put your theoretical knowledge into practice?

Do you ignore theoretical safety standards at work?

CRITERION-REFERENCED VERSUS TRADITIONAL MEASUREMENT

I first heard about 'mastery learning' in 1978 when I read W James Popham's book *Criterion-referenced Measurement* (1978). Popham exposed a fundamental flaw in traditional assessment where everyone is measured against everyone else studying the subject with no absolute reference to the range and quality of subject knowledge and practice. High grades in traditional exams mean that you are better than other people taking the exam: it does not necessarily mean that you are good at the subject. When the principle aim of an examination is to 'spread 'em out' so that you can grade the learners, you do not ask questions which everyone will get right.

Popham used the terms 'criterion-referenced measurement' and 'mastery learning' as two names for the same thing. Since that time many other related terms have come into circulation, such as 'competency-based' assessment and 'performance-based' criteria. Some may see subtle differences between the terms and wish for different definitions but essentially we are dealing with the same thing. Here is a general rule:

> Somebody decides the standards which have to be achieved before an award can be given to an individual.

The 'somebody' is usually a panel of expert examiners or, in the case of the UK National Vocational Qualifications, a National Lead Body for an occupational area drawn from industry, the professions, commerce or trade, and educationalists, trade unionists and/or trainers working with validating and awarding bodies. These standards are taken from current industrial or professional practice and are defined together with the conditions under which the performance will be carried out. An individual competes against set standards, not against other learners. Rights of access, fair assessment and equal opportunities are guaranteed for all who can benefit from the programme.

Components of a skill

Every skill contains the three types of knowing which were described in Chapter 1: knowing 'that', knowing 'how' and knowing 'what ought to be done'. Figure 3.1 shows the three factors as different dimensions of a performance; every vocational and occupational performance will have a different emphasis.

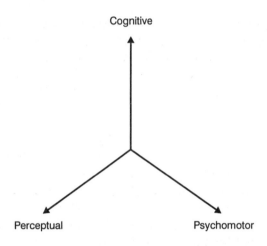

Figure 3.1 *The components of a performance*

The skill of a lawyer will be high in cognitive and affective knowledge and fairly low in psychomotor skills, whereas a ballet dancer's performance will show high intelligence in bodily control but a lesser cognitive content.

Example: Cooking

Cognitive – basic chemical and physiological understanding of proteins, carbohydrates, fats, vitamins, minerals, the role of water and fibre, the de-naturing of proteins by heat, the growth of micro-organisms, anatomy and physiology.
Psychomotor – cooking skills of boiling, braising, stewing, baking, texture construction like the scrambling of eggs or the creation of soufflés, knife-handling skills for slicing vegetables, skinning fish or chopping meat, use of equipment.

Perceptual – colour, texture and presentation of food, empathy for those with eating disorders such as obesity and anorexia nervosa, sensitive approach for the very young, the elderly and the sick. The cultural importance of traditional foods and recipes with seasonal variations.

========= **ACTIVITY** =========

Components in one of your performance assessments.
Select a performance that you assess. It may be one for which you have to make your own assessment plan or you may have clear pre-set criteria which have to be met. Make a table of the component skills by answering the following questions:

- What is the performance that you are assessing?
- What is the cognitive knowledge which has to be demonstrated?
- What psychomotor skills must be used, to what standard and under which conditions?
- What judgements of quality will have to be made about the final product?
- Which interpersonal sensitivities are important in the practice of this performance?

ALL OR NOTHING

There are no grades within competency-based assessment. All the assessor has to judge is whether competence has been achieved and whether there is enough evidence of underpinning knowledge. The standard to be achieved is so carefully defined that the learner either has the competence or has not yet achieved it. If an awarding body wishes to judge a higher stage of competence and deeper understanding, then another set of standards has to be defined and the learner attempts to achieve a higher level. Providing evidence of competence is an all-or-nothing process.

This is a very difficult concept to grasp in criterion-referenced testing, and can seem harsh. You can perform or you cannot. This competence has to be current and competences which you possessed when you were younger do not count. There seems to be a sentimental trend in education today to blur the edges of such a decision. Incompetent and unable people are carried along by teachers with unrealistic evaluations of abilities. This lack of realism seems kind and egalitarian but in reality it is harmful: the person is being sheltered from the truth.

Life is no respecter of sensitive egos. At sea, for example, when you claim to have tied a proper bowline but fail to do so, the wind, waves or boat motion will undo the false knot in a flash and your self-deception is exposed. False emotions are equally easy to detect. After a week of stormy conditions in the close proximity of a small boat, the crew end up loving or hating each other.

Assessment that tests physical ability can be hard for an individual to accept. take the example of a merchant naval officer or a civil aircraft pilot, who has to show a competence which involves perfect eyesight; older and highly-experienced sailors and pilots have to renew their certificate of competence. Would you ignore the fact that a man or a woman overcame the physical changes of age by using contact lenses when these were not allowed for new candidates? What about learners with physical or mental barriers to learning? No assessor can sign-off a person as competent if they fail to meet all the necessary criteria. In a recent article in a national newspaper, an education journalist claimed that competency-based assessment was an easy option because an assessor could tick off a list of competences without bothering to check the learner's performance. I was horrified that she used 'Competency at sea' as her example and claimed that her sailing assessor had agreed she was competent at several practical sailing skills when she was not. This silly woman is now a danger to all who sail with her and the practical sailing assessor ought to be struck off the awarding body panel. This journalist was openly prepared to admit that she cheated in the test of competence, but it is most unlikely that she would admit to cheating in a formal examination.

In the UK GNVQs (General National Vocational Qualifications) are based on a similar competence model but are designed for learners who are still at school. There are problems with establishing assessment procedures for candidates who do not have proven competence in the workplace (see page 110). In general, school and college students have to prove their ability to *achieve* the required competencies; evidence shows the potential to achieve working competence.

POSITIVE ACTIONS

Competency-based assessment involves positive actions which may not be demanded in traditional assessment. D O Hebb (1949) distinguished between intelligence A, intelligence B and intelligence C:

Intelligence A – the theoretical knowledge and understanding which is held within the individual's own internal thinking system. This is the working memory, functional and procedural processes, 'day-dreaming and fantasy' (described in Books 1 and 2).
Intelligence B – the application of theoretical knowledge and procedures which can be observed in deliberate, individual behaviour, and the public expression of specialist knowledge in intelligence A; the 'public' self which is open to examination systems, both traditional and competency-based.
Intelligence C – the public and visible expression of common sense. This is a demonstration of physical, interpersonal and intrapersonal skills with wise decision making which expresses the multiple intelligence described by Gardner (1985).

Because competency-based assessment requires the learner to demonstrate both intelligence B and intelligence C, it demands positive actions which may commit, or appear to commit, the learner to underlying social and moral values.

Social learning and social acceptability play an important part in occupational employment and sometimes it is difficult to sort out practical guidelines from the underlying principles.

ACTIVITY

Constraints on criterion-referenced testing.

Your assessment may focus on the production of a quality product but even the most apparently harmless performances can raise fundamental issues; for example, is it fair to lay down compulsory assessment in cooking in which a vegetarian has to handle animal flesh? Think through some of the criterion-referenced assessment that you have to cover and work out if there are any moral or value judgements involved.

THE NATURE OF EVIDENCE

Although the assessment of underpinning knowledge can be carried out in group tests and workshop practice can be marked while several people are working together, the bulk of criterion-referenced assessment has to be done individually. There are four main rules which are the basis of this individual assessment task and the assessor must be sure that each rule is covered by the evidence:

Is it your work?	authenticity
When did you do it?	currency
Have you covered all the criteria?	comprehensiveness
Did you really do it, not pretend?	validity

Authenticity

When you stand with a checklist and watch someone perform a skill there is little doubt about authenticity, but project work and group reports can have all sorts of freeloaders. I have always been especially careful when judging witness statements or reports from work experience as it is essential to have documentary evidence of reliability and qualifications when accepting other peoples' statements of the competence achieved. If you have any doubts, interview the candidate; even if this has to be done over the telephone you can get some first-hand clues as to the genuineness of the evidence.

Currency

The assessor has to be very careful and tactful when checking up on currency. When the skill-training certificate is more than two years old there must be evidence of current practice and additional certificates of retesting where necessary. Skills and competences are so much part of a person's self-image that a test of the currency of dearly-held competence is highly personal and potentially very damaging. It is like assessing the flexibility of an ageing ballet dancer or the manual dexterity of an elderly fiddle player: technique can mask a multitude of physical deteriorations but it is inevitable that old muscles will wear out. The rules of competency-based assessment are tough and, if you cannot perform nowadays, you have not got the competency. I have used the example of aging but any other cause of physical deterioration has to be treated in the same way. Many certificates of competence are the basis of safety regulations for other people and it is not fair on those people if an assessor of competence is kind-hearted to an ageing or otherwise deteriorating person.

Comprehensiveness

In traditional assessment, coverage of the range and depth of work is usually achieved by random sampling and in some forms of examination, question spotting from one year to the next is an advanced art form. This is not permitted in criterion-referenced testing and the learner has to produce evidence of *all* parts and range of competence. The assessor, and especially the verifier, may choose to sample the evidence but all evidence must be submitted.

There is another side to this rule of assessment and that is the exclusion from assessment of any part which is *not* stated in the original standard. In criterion-referenced measurement it is unacceptable to try to assess outside the criteria laid down.

Validity

In Chapter 6, which covers the important subject of reliability and validity, all these rules which are important to criterion-referenced testing will be discussed. They must be borne in mind when discussing the type of evidence which is needed.

GATHERING EVIDENCE

The competency-based approach has forced a great change in education and training, bringing freedom for the individual but also a great responsibility. The task of assessment has shifted from teachers, trainers and examiners to the learner. Evidence of competence is shown in the workplace as a skilled performance or professional practice, not as well-written examination scripts. Assessment of competence is highly invidual – an excellent principle because each person can be confident that qualifications are a true record of their work and achievement. However, it is not possible to assign one assessor to record all the progress of an individual during the process of his or her work, so the responsibility of gathering evidence falls on the individual learner.

In many ways the collection of evidence to prove competency is like a fine arts student gathering together a portfolio of work to display to potential sponsors. The learner has to demonstrate the range and extent of his or her skill, knowledge and performance. They have to make sure that the portfolio contains sufficient evidence for every aspect to be covered. Although the evidence has to include all parts of the set criteria, unlike a traditional examination where the learner can elect to demonstrate knowledge of a limited number of topics by choice from an examination paper, evidence which is not relevant must be excluded. It is for the learner, not the assessor, to realize what evidence is relevant to cover the standards of competency.

Assessors must not accept evidence which is outside the specific competences which are being assessed. There is a terrible temptation for learners to submit massive files of evidence which is unsifted and uncatalogued. Because each individual's work is in a unique package, it is not possible to use a standard marking plan as in traditional assessment, and not at all possible to use a computer marking system which can be a feature of standard tests. All the criteria have to be covered, so the assessment is largely a matter of making sure that all the evidence is complete. It takes about one hour to assess one unit in the NVQ system, but if the assessor starts to search for evidence in an undifferentiated and disorganized file, this can extend to several hours, even with the help of the learner, in a portfolio assessment tutorial. Part of the skill of being competent is to be organized, so the assessor must *not* be conned by a plausible student into doing the evidence-gathering.

Gathering evidence is a skill which has to be learned, in the same way as there are skills to be acquired in taking examinations. Some people are disadvantaged by test anxiety and make a poor showing in a formal examination. A portfolio of evidence to prove personal competence would include factors such as:

- recognition of prior learning and experience for accreditation
- note-taking and word-processing ability
- organization of paperwork and cross-referencing
- understanding standards and competency statements
- asking appropriate people for witness statements
- following a personal action plan
- presenting evidence of progress in review sessions
- personal communication skills in the spoken and written word
- graphic skills such as lay-out
- clear understanding of long-term personal development

● overview of how a particular qualification will enhance individual progress.

It can be argued that all these skills are essential for holding down a job; they are certainly not the same as the ability to overcome writer's cramp in a hot, crowded examination room.

The skills required by competency-based assessment are beginning to be taught in British schools with the introduction of General National Vocational Qualifications (GNVQs) and they fit in very well with the move towards National Vocational Qualifications in the trained workforce and continuous professional development (CPD) which is becoming an essential part of many professional workers' careers. The ability to recognize and record experience as a natural part of life is the key feature of competency-based assessment.

The consequence of this shift towards natural performance as the basis of personal qualifications has advantages and disadvantages over an artificial and concentrated effort in the examination room. All the wasted effort and loss of talent which used to occur when highly selected candidates were failed in the final stages of qualification is a thing of the past. There are no 'BA (Failed)' people now because it is possible to turn all experience into some form of evidence for competency-based qualifications but, on the other hand, it is more difficult to hide periods of indifferent work. Developments in information technology make vast record storage possible so that it is now possible to have a national record which contains every detail of progress in our careers.

Evidence gathering methods

Observation of work practices and behaviour

This is normally called 'natural observation in the workplace' and is regarded as the best way to produce evidence of competence. In the professions this type of evidence is proof of professional competence. Skilled crafts and trades place importance on high performance in the workplace. These are the stages of the process:

- Agree an assessment plan, making clear what competences are to be assessed, which assessment method is to be used, under which conditions and to which criteria. This assessment plan should be signed and agreed by the learner and the assessor.
- Arrange for an observer: make sure the witness or assessor has a copy of the assessment plan, details of the criteria which are to be assessed, an observation checklist and prepared questions to assess underpinning knowledge.
- Observe the performance: the assessor must record the learner's performance on the observation checklist and be as unobtrusive as possible during the observation. This is *not* a time for teaching and if the observer makes suggestions or interferes with the performance, the learner must automatically be recorded as 'not yet achieved competency'.
- Assess underpinning knowledge: the assessor asks appropriate questions about underpinning knowledge and the reasons behind practical procedures. It is important that the observer is a subject specialist so that a proper judgement can be made in the assessment.
- Make an assessment decision: the assessor decides whether or not the learner has achieved the performance criteria and shown underpinning knowledge. The assessor must not take anything else into account other than the agreed competences described in the assessment plan. Feedback should be constructive and helpful and decisions should be given as quickly as possible. When a learner is not signed off as having achieved the competency then he or she should be told that they have 'not yet achieved competency' and the assessor should work with the learner to see how competency can be reached. Because there is no 'grade of passing', an assessor cannot predict that a candidate will not achieve competence at a future date. Employers and funding authorities may impose a time deadline for

a candidate, in which case there can be a failure to achieve competence in a given time, but without such a constraint, a competency test can never be failed.

- Record and link with verification: all assessment plans, observation checklists, records of verbal questions together with written feedback are evidence which must be collated within the learner's portfolio. The assessor should then record the assessment decision so that the process of internal and external verification can begin, this quality control system is described on page 125.

The use of simulation in the workplace

Many assessors assume that all evidence should come from the workplace and that simulation should be avoided. This attitude stems from the early days of criterion-referenced testing when the college, in particular, tried to carry out all assessment by simulation. Now the progress of virtual reality has enabled great advances in graphic training by simulation so that highly critical, but rare events, can be made available to all trainees. It is possible to simulate jet flight and include some of the most rare decisions which may occur. This development has caused a change in attitude towards evidence which is produced from simulation. As a general rule, any action which is critical to the job, like the giving of injections to patients in nurse training, must be witnessed on the job. The same conditions apply to evidence for any task which has to be undertaken frequently. Simulation can be considered for any operation, critical or non-critical, which is rare in the normal work situation. This means that crises, like realistic fire drills, can use the new simulation techniques to produce evidence of competence.

Choosing a witness

Evidence of performance, whether simulated or real, can be given by any outside observer: clients, colleagues or managers. The decision about what weight to give to witness statements rests with the subject matter specialist who is part of the assessment centre team (see page 122). To help the assessor weigh the evidence of a witness statement fairly, the learner should provide a 'status' report for any outside witness. A nice report from a loyal mum may not be given the same weight as a report from an experienced work-based observer.

Other evidence

Because competency-based assessment is relatively new, many traditional teachers and trainers assume that only evidence of performance can be given; this limits the validity of the assessment to fairly simple craft subjects. However, there is no reason why sophisticated skills and knowledge cannot be assessed by criterion-referenced testing provided that sound evidence is put forward. Here is a list of techniques which can be used in criterion-referenced testing of advanced knowledge:

- complex simulation systems, including computer models and virtual reality
- questioning, both written and oral, to assess underpinning knowledge
- case study, role play and syndicates
- statements of reflection or intent
- assignments, projects, decision making or problem solving
- evidence gathered as a continuous process during work.

Chapter 4

Standard Tests

 CONCEPTS

Standard answers
Psychological testing
Psychometric testing
Personality questionnaires
Objective tests
Assessment on demand

STANDARD ANSWERS

Standard tests cannot exist unless there are standard answers. Every item in an intelligence test has one 'correct' answer which is acceptable to the person who wrote the test. Each multiple-choice item has a stem (the correct response) concealed amid the distracters. Sometimes one response will indicate certain characteristics or trends while another will point to something different. Choose one response in a questionnaire and you might indicate that you are an extrovert, a natural leader, a liar, an active learner, or responsive to TV advertising; choose the other response and you become an introvert, a subordinate, truthful, a reflective learner or resistant to TV advertising.

Every standard test represents the test writer's theory. The writer of an intelligence test assumes that intelligent people will choose certain answers and a psychological tester hypothesizes that people with some personality traits will choose one set of responses whilst people of a different type will choose another set. My instinct is to resent these testers assuming they can try out their theories on a unique person like me but this is to be sentimental in the face of large numbers. There are two reasons why standard tests appear to be accurate and supply useful information about individual:

- when a very large number of people are measured by the same test, individual differences are ironed out and clear general trends appear;
- when each item or response within a questionnaire is checked to make sure that it points clearly to the general trend of the test, the whole questionnaire is strengthened as a measure of the tester's theory.

PSYCHOLOGICAL TESTING

There is a sense in which all assessment can be regarded as psychological testing, even when we simply ask each other questions, but all standard testing is clearly psychological. When decisions affecting career prospects are taken it is essential that every effort is made to produce fair standard testing methods. In the UK, the British Psychological Society takes responsibility for setting standards in the administration and regulation of such testing. Trainers and managers must ensure that standard psychological tests are administered by qualified testers. This applies to all tests of aptitude, including all intelligence tests as well as personality tests. Even market researchers using questionnaires in the High Street need training in the methods of approaching the general public.

Many commercial, trade and professional organizations set entry qualifications which may be achieved by special written examinations or are defined by minimum levels of achievement at school, college or university. Some organizations have complex entry tests which may include:

psychometric tests,
standardized interviews,
observed group discussion,
observed social behaviour,
tests of problem solving within a group,
tests of leadership in group tasks,
tests of practical procedures.

⇨ **STOP AND REFLECT** ⇦

Do you think that such tests are against personal rights?

Intelligence is a factor assessed in some psychological tests; are you happy that such personal data should be held by a commercial organization?

Are all interviewers and assessors properly trained?

I am concerned about the right of people like employers, or health workers, to use standard tests and I am especially concerned about the confidentiality of the information gathered. Could you be forced, for example, to want employment so much that you dare not question a potential employer's methods and actions?

The British Psychological Society (BPS) has a key role in controlling the publication of professionally-produced test materials (Toplis *et al.*, 1987).

This is the way in which the BPS defines a test:

- a procedure for the evaluation of psychological functions, intelligence; ability; aptitude; language development and function; perception; personality; temperament and disposition; and interests, habits, values and preferences
- those being tested are involved in solving problems, performing skilled tasks or making judgements. Some results may may be interpreted qualitatively by reference to psychological theory

- test procedures are characterized by standard methods of administration and scoring, and highly controlled and uniform procedures are defined. For example, the first items are easy so that weaker candidates can settle into the test more easily; the items get more difficult as the test proceeds
- results are usually quantified by means of normative or other scaling procedures (see Chapter 5 for statistical procedures). When the raw score for a test has been made it does not mean very much on its own unless it is compared to the results of a large number of other people who have taken the same test. By doing this check against average results it is possible to say if the individual score is higher, lower or about the same as the normal population.

PSYCHOMETRIC TESTING

Here is a list of some psychometric techniques

Tests of attainment

These are the school, college, university, trade and professional examinations used at every stage in education and training and in every occupational area.

Tests of general intelligence

A simple definition of general intelligence might be 'the capacity for abstract thinking and reasoning'. Many ingenious tests have been created but the most reliable are the ones which are used for a very large number of people and in which each item has been honed to assess what the test writer wishes to measure.

Verbal ability

Tests of verbal ability range from simple tests of meaning and comprehension to the sort of lexicographical test which would confound a code breaker.

Numerical ability

It is possible to list the ability to use numbers in a hierarchy and come very close to an absolute scale of mathematical ability. Cronbach (1984) researched this area of assessment in an attempt to create a system of overlapping tests which were free from any applied content. He called this absolute scale of mathematical ability 'mathematical wits'!

Mechanical ability

Questions are usually in the form of diagrams which show a situation. The candidate is expected to work through a series of subsequent events and decide what will happen next. It is difficult to find items which do not rely on some previous experience of engineering.

A typical diagram would show a series of pulleys linked by a rope. The question might ask which direction one of the pulleys would move when the rope was pulled.

Spatial ability

Spatial ability seems to be closely linked with left- and right-hand side of the brain activity. Some people seem to be able to think in 3D whereas others appear to be mental flat-earthers.

═══════════════ **ACTIVITY** ═══════════════

A spatial ability item on surface development.
Each item consists of a drawing of a piece of paper which could be folded to form the object shown beside it. Part of the object has been shaded. You are to shade the corresponding area of the flat piece of paper. There is no shading on surfaces you cannot see. Look at the example below which has been correctly completed:

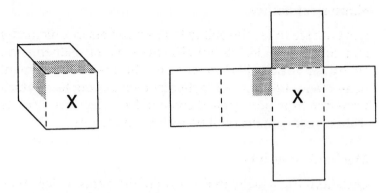

All of the flat pieces of paper have been marked with an X
This X also shows on the completed object. Here is one
for you to try:

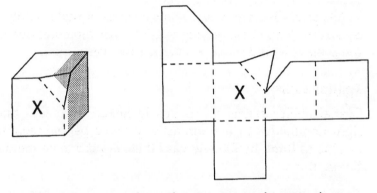

This is an extract from the Garnett Multi-aptitude test.
Check your solution with the answer at the end of the
chapter.

Manual dexterity or eye–hand coordination

Although many tests of manual skills are devised for
special occasions, there are not many widely recognized,
standardized tests. One which is commonly used and
which can be justified is the Crawford Manual Dexterity
Test which is used in the selection of dental technicians.

The candidate is allowed to practise so that any variations in experience can be reduced, then the time taken to perform two simple manual tasks is recorded.

ACTIVITY

Create your own manual dexterity test.
Restriction of access to courses and assessment barriers to qualification are much easier to justify in the area of manual dexterity. If a person cannot perform manual dexterity skills within a set time and to a particular standard then there is no justification in allowing that person on to a training programme. Similarly, if a person cannot complete the final competences in a programme because of a failure to show the necessary manual dexterity then no qualification should be given. Decisions are clear-cut and easier to make than in the cognitive domain. If you are responsible for some type of manual skill training, create a pre-programme skills test which you can give to all applicants.

PERSONALITY QUESTIONNAIRES

The term 'personality' covers all aspects of the way an individual interacts with the environment. Questionnaires on personality characteristics assess factors such as emotional adjustment, social relations, motivation, interests, values and attitudes. The format is often a self-assessment with a large number of questions aimed at certain characteristics. I find my students enjoy finding out about themselves but I am not sure that they take any more notice of the conclusions than they would from a questionnaire in a magazine.

Eysenck Personality Inventory (EPI)

This questionnaire is widely used in research and is regarded as a robust measurement of personality type. The term 'robust' is used when a test has been shown to be reliable and valid over a long period and with a wide population. There are 24 questions for a stable – neurotic dimension and another 24 questions for an introvert – extrovert dimension. The remaining questions are used to establish the honesty of the responses to allow for the fact that some people may want to impress the tester. These 'lie' questions are easy to detect once you know that they are concealed in the test.

One interesting feature of the Eysenck Inventory is that when the two scores are cross-referenced, personality falls into the four ancient categories of: sanguine, phlegmatic, melancholic and choleric. I arrange for my students to score their own forms because it helps them to understand the structure of the questionnaire. Once we were all busy calculating our scores when there was an explosion from the middle of the group and a red-faced man with bright blue eyes yelled out, 'I've come out *choleric!*' All my dear students held their breath for about 10 seconds before collapsing in great laughter. The EPI is a very robust test.

Cattell's 16 Personality Factor (16PF)

This personality questionnaire is widely used in industry, but I have found that trainers and managers have a poor grasp of the theory behind the test. Eyscenck plotted personality like the four points of a compass: North – extrovert, South – introvert; East – neurotic, West – stable, so that a person could be analysed as being extrovert and stable or extrovert and neurotic, for example. Cattell's theory is nothing like as simple. He put forward 16 different scales for personality which make a total of 32 different characteristics. They are not separate, like North–South, East–West, but they all interrelate and overlap. Whereas Eysenck has 24 questions which relate to each scale, the 16PF is much longer but there are only six or eight questions for each personality scale.

In my experience, 16PF is much less robust. It is especially vulnerable to cultural differences. I used it in India and the dimension of group-dependent versus group-independent proved ineffective. This is quite in line with the theory because the test was standardized for the British population; however, I found the same difficulty when I used the test for British students of Indian extraction. It is important to remember that human beings do not operate like chemicals in a test tube and all assessment should be carried out by testers who understand the theory behind the test instrument. Managers and trainers should not buy human tests off the shelf and expect to make reliable and sensible decisions in human relations.

Interest questionnaires

Questionnaires are designed for vocational and career guidance purposes as well as for selection. Super and Crites (1962) divided out:

- *expressed interest* – when an individual states a preference
- *manifest interest* – when an individual voluntarily participates
- *inventoried interest* – measured by tests which compare interests in different activities.

These inventories may divide interest into areas, such as medicine, engineering, music and business, and then divide the areas into levels:

professional – with full academic and practical training
semi-professional – requiring some advanced training
supervisory – high degrees of competence on the job
skilled – requiring competency training
unskilled – requiring basic training.

It is interesting that these levels correspond exactly to the NVQ levels which are described on page 112.

Attitude questionnaires

Over 60 years ago, Rensis Likert (1932) developed a successful way of measuring attitudes which can also be used as an observational checklist. The attitude measure usually consists of a statement, followed by the choice between say:

strongly approve
approve
undecided
disapprove
strongly disapprove

Each scale has to be prepared by a panel of experts who first decide which statements consistently indicate a particular attitude and which 'pole' – strongly approve or strongly disapprove – represents that attitude. The statements are mixed randomly so that the candidate does not get into the habit of ticking down the left-hand side or the right-hand side of the scale. A score can be devised by marking the pole 5 points: approve, disapprove: 4, undecided: 3, and so on

Likert scales are affected by individual personality: some people are quick and decided in their opinions and others waiver and often go for the undecided verdict, so that some people will score down either side of the scale and others will tend to tick in the middle.

ACTIVITY

Some items for a Likert attitude scale.

Pick a topic, say attitude to women, and write some statements which will highlight this attitude:for example, 'A woman's place is in the home'. Decide the polarity of the statement; in our case people with a positive attitude to women would strongly disagree. It is helpful to consult one or two colleagues about the statements before arranging to try out your questionnaire.

It is easy to change an attitudinal scale into an observational checklist on attitudes. For example, the assessor might want to measure a care assistant's attitude to patients and so the item would read:

The care assistant's attitude to the patient was:
5 – thoughtful and considerate at all times
4 – generally considerate
3 – often considerate
2 – sometimes considerate
1 – detached, inconsiderate

When writing this type of Likert scale it is important that the five alternatives measure attitudes along the same dimension. It would not be possible to use a scale if the items had said:

5 – thoughtful and considerate at all times
4 – highly competent and skilled
3 – cheerful and jolly
2 – physically incapable of lifting the patient
1 – such a strong body odour that the patient recoiled

because each of these alternatives could have been observed but they do not belong to homogeneous group of choices. Cheerful attitudes would have to be compared with other moods and physical weaknesses with physical strengths.

Many years ago I used to carry out teaching observation armed with nearly 100 items on the Garnett Observation Scale. Some of the items were quite fun and would include things like:

Is the chalkboard work. . .?	*Is the voice. . .?*
5 – consistently legible and neat	5 – outstanding
4 – usually a good standard	4 – effectively modulated
3 – inconsistently organized	3 – modulated
2 – sometimes disorganized	2 – monotonous
1 – illegible and disorganized	1 – unpleasant

OBJECTIVE TESTS

Objective questions are so called because

- they are written to test specified learning outcomes
- no subjective judgement is required to mark them
- they are based on verifiable facts or principles
- their content is chosen objectively.

Multiple-choice items are the most popular type in objective testing. Each item consists of three parts: a stem, a key and a number of distracters. The key and distracters together are often referred to as options. The stem can be either a direct question or an incomplete statement; the key is the correct answer and the distracters are plausible but incorrect answers.

ACTIVITY

Writing a multiple-choice item.
I find a useful way is to create a 'Harvard Square' out of two dichotomies which are relevant to the question; this produces three nicely balanced distracters to go with the key (correct response). Here is an example to look at before you have a go yourself:

What is the perfect radiating surface?

	Matt	Shiny
White	MATT and WHITE	SHINY and WHITE
Black	MATT and BLACK (the 'key')	SHINY and BLACK

Now try to work out a multiple-choice question using the same technique.

Other objective items include:

- *Multiple response* – where the candidate selects a group of answers from a list of suggestions. This type is useful, for example, in picking out metals from a list of chemical elements.
- *Matching block* – where the candidate has to match listed examples to different types. This pairing of examples with cases can make a useful test for reminding learners about the ideas in the previous learning session.
- *Assertion. . .Reason* – this specialized item in which two statements are linked by the word 'because' can be used to test advanced levels of understanding and logic. The item is suited to subjects such as law, management and philosophy and gives the lie to those who say that objective tests are suited only to low levels of work.
- *True or false* – simple statements are made and the candidate has to state whether they are true of false. Useful when massed together for quick recapping or recall.
- *Completion* – gaps in writing which the learner has to fill. These are not strictly objective because the learner has to supply the answer from a list rather than come up with the answer themself, but they are good questions for helping recall.

Short questions are much in favour in standard tests these days and have the following characteristics:

- they are at the opposite end of the spectrum from open-ended, essay questions
- they attempt to ask questions requiring exact answers
- they usually take less than five minutes to read and answer; many take less than a minute
- they include some guidance on the extent of the answer required, eg the area of blank paper in the answer space

or specific instructions such as, 'In not more than 20 words. . .'.

━━━━━━━━━━ **ACTIVITY** ━━━━━━━━━━

Avoiding mistakes in writing multiple-choice items.
In Australia I found a splendid 'content-free' objective test on a photocopier. My sub-editor found it 'irrelevant and annoying, with childish overtones', but you may like to try it anyway because I have found it useful for people who write objective test items! (My comments are given at the end of this chapter.)

Look for the clues – a content-free test

Select one – only one answer is correct. Spend not more than 15 minutes in total on the test.

1. The usual function of a grunge-proker is to remove
   A Grunges
   B Snarts
   C Trigs
   D Grods

2. Antigrottification occurs
   A On spring mornings
   B On summer evenings provided there is no rain before dusk
   C On autumn afternoons
   D On winter nights

3. Lurkies suffer from trangitis because
   A Their prads are always underdeveloped
   B All their brises are horizontal
   C Their curnpieces are usually imperfect
   D None of their dringes can ever adapt

4. Non-responsive frattling is usually found in an
   A Gringle
   B Janket
   C Kloppie
   D Uckerpod

5. Which are the exceptions to the law of lompicality
   A The miltrip and the nattercup
   B The bifid pantrip
   C The common queeter
   D The flanged ozzer

6. Which must be present for parbling to take place
   A Phlot and runge
   B Runge
   C The common queeter and runge
   D Runge and trake

7. One common disorder of an over-spragged ucker pod is
   A Copious vezzling
   B Intermittent weggerment
   C Non-responsive frattling
   D Uneven yerkation

8. Which of these is to the right: A, B, C, D?

An objective test specification

Objective test items are written to a test specification which has already been decided by the examiners. In 1968 I was an examiner for the City and Guilds of London Institute course, Science Laboratory Technicians, when it was decided to introduce an objective test. We were invited to write items for the test at the rate of 75p an item plus another 25p if the item was incorporated into the bank of questions. It was rather fun and we were asked to add to our suggestions with:

– a syllabus reference

– an indication whether the item tested knowledge, comprehension, application or evaluation of the subject reference.

The items were vetted by an editorial panel of three examiners before they were tried out for their balance and effectiveness. Here is an example of test specification:

Syllabus	Knowledge	Comprehension	Application	Total
Topic A	9	2	1	12
Topic B	3	8	3	14
Topic C	7	3	2	12
Topic D	8	1	2	11
Topic E	2	7	2	11
Total	29	21	10	60

At one minute each for 60 items the test lasts 60 minutes.

Subject experts decide the weighting of subject areas across the syllabus, number the subject matter areas and the type of knowledge to be assessed. This process of test specification means that, unlike traditional essay-type examinations, the whole range of the syllabus can be covered and the same balance of questioning can be produced everytime.

ASSESSMENT ON DEMAND

When the item bank contains plenty of questions which have been checked for suitability, it is possible to produce standard tests on demand. New items have to be checked for reliability and validity before they are placed in the bank and a safe way of checking is to run a few extra new items each time the test is used. This clever but simple method ensures that all new items are validated by the right target population – the people who take the test – and under the right test conditions. New items do not affect the test results for the candidate and this is a reliable way to get individual item statistics. (More on statistics and reliability in the next two chapters.)

Solution to the spatial ability item:

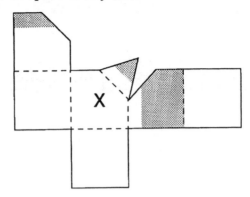

Comments on the content-free test:

This test provides examples of the mistakes which must be avoided when writing multiple choice items.

Q.1 The stem which contains 'grunge-prokers' gives away the key, which is 'grunges'.

Q.2 All the responses are short except one which is much longer.

Q.3 All the responses are definite except one which is qualified. Absolute statements are rarely correct because there is always likely to be at least one exception.

Q.4 This is an English grammar error. The stem ends with 'an' and there is only one response which begins with a vowel.

Q.5 Another English grammar error. In the stem, the verb 'are' is used so the answer must be more than one.

Q.6 Logical error. As 'runge' appears in all possible answers and the stem asks for 'which must be present', there can be only one correct answer.

Q.7 This is given away by an earlier question – number 4.

Q.8 An invalid question if ever there was one! Which letter is on the right of the others? D.

And the whole test is invalid because there is a clear pattern about the responses viz: A, B, C, D. A, B, C, D. The correct responses should be random in reliable test construction.

Chapter 5

Statistics and Records

 CONCEPTS

The use of statistics
Scales of measurement
Descriptive statistical techniques
Inferential statistical techniques
Recording

THE USE OF STATISTICS

That comment about lies, damned lies and statistics is most
unfair to statistics because it is the fools in charge of statistics that are the liars. As a tool, statistics are most helpful
and all trainers and teachers need to know some of the
basic principles if only to confront those people who lie
with statistics. The use of computers has revolutionized
every aspect of statistical procedure and has made the
keeping of records much easier and more systematic.

There are standard and agreed ways of calculating and
presenting data which are designed to put forward an
honest and truthful record. Of course, some detail is lost if
complicated masses of numbers are represented in a
simplified form. What is and what is not 'statistically signif-

icant' has a precise meaning and you may wonder if statistical significance is necessary. You may say, 'Let the facts speak for themselves' and in the physical sciences this statement is likely to make good sense; when living organisms are involved this simple approach is not a good course. There are so many factors when you deal with plants, animals and humans that the 'plain facts' do not stand out and it is very difficult to draw clear results. Think about the number of different factors which may affect learning in a study of different teaching and learning strategies. When dealing with data about people, the need for statistics is vital and presentation and the inferences drawn from the data must follow the honest rules laid down by statistical procedures.

There are two types of statistics which are useful to the teacher and trainer:

- descriptive statistics, and
- inferential statistics.

Descriptive Statistics

Whenever your purpose is merely to describe a set of data, you are engaged in employing descriptive statistics. The NVQ results from 1995, the number of students in higher education, and certain grades on an examination in a particular course, are all examples of descriptive statistics.

Descriptive statistics are most important in assessment and have a wealth of techniques like histograms and bar charts, and important measures, such as means, variances and standard deviation – all essential to an understanding of inferential statistics.

Inferential Statistics

Most of the statistical work in evaluation is concerned with inferential statistics. The concepts of populations and samples are important because inferential statistics is concerned with using samples to infer something about whole populations. We have to know if changes and new techniques have resulted in a genuine improvement; is the change statistically significant?

SCALES OF MEASUREMENT

Nominal Scales

In a sense nominal scales are not really scales at all, since they do not scale items along any dimension, but rather label them. An example of a nominal scale is the set of numbers assigned to rugby players. Sometimes these numbers have no meaning whatsoever other than as convenient labels distinguishing the players from one another.

These scales are used exclusively in criterion-referenced testing. The performance criteria and range statements are clearly defined before the assessment starts and most validating bodies define the assessment as well. When the learner is assessed against these standards, the standards are either achieved or they are not. At the end of the assessment the learner is labelled as someone who has the competency or has not got the competency. This is a nominal statistic even if the name, which can include a number of performance criteria and a range statement, is rather a long one.

The use of nominal scales can be seen as a threat to trainers. If the training programme is sound and the trainers are effective then all learners ought to achieve competence. When they do not, blame will fall equally on the programme and the trainers as well as on the learner. Schools of motoring make a good example. On any day at the driving test centre potentially everyone can pass or everyone can fail because the learner drivers are competing against the driving test regulations and not each other. If you run a driving school and all your learners pass, then you may feel you have a good programme and effective trainers. If all fail, you look to the learning strategies and the methods of instruction first. It is only later that you worry about recruiting a 'better type' of learner driver.

⇨ **STOP AND REFLECT** ⇦

Because competency-based assessment is measured, and very often funded, by successful achievement, do you think this puts undue pressure on trainers to 'get the candidate through at all costs?'

Do you think that this payment by results affects selection for training programmes even though they are thought to be 'open to all who will benefit'?

Do you think trainers have less job security because the nominal scale is used in competency assessment?

Ordinal scale

The simplest true scale is an ordinal scale, which rank orders people, objects or events along some continuum; this is best, next best, number three and so on, like the runners in a race. No attempt is made to assess the gap between places, like differences in times, because there are no numbers or amounts in ordinal scales. There are no indications as to how close the finish.

In education there may be social and ethical objections to this type of scale but it does reflect what happens to people in the competitive working world. It is odd therefore that in many research projects teachers have been shown to be very accurate in their opinions when they have been asked to predict the rank order of their class. Even with large numbers in a group teachers seem to be able to forecast the rank of success very accurately.

It is easy for one teacher to rank his or her learners quite accurately but errors creep in when these ranks are combined between different teachers and the accurate ranks are expressed as teachers' marks. This is the notorious difficulty of cross-assessor marking.

Let us use a simple model of three teachers A, B and C, each with a class of four students. The three classes of students are 'matched', that is, each group of four has been chosen because they each have the same spread of ability. All the teachers are good at their job and they can rank their classes accurately, so in each case they have a clear best student who comes first, closely followed by a second good student, the next able is placed third and then the least able is number four, the weakest of the group. In all three groups the teachers have ranked:

1st A	2nd A	3rd A	Last A
1st B	2nd B	3rd B	Last B
1st C	2nd C	3rd C	Last C

Now let us say that each teacher sets the same test to all 12 students and marks that test out of a total of 10 marks. The first teacher is an average marker and awards the marks to class A in the following way:

1st A	2nd A	3rd A	Last A
7	6	4	3

The second teacher believes in encouragement marking but sticks to the same good ranking by awarding:

1st B	2nd B	3rd B	Last B
10	9	7	6

The third teacher in C class is fair but firm and likes to make the group work hard for rather mean encouragement:

1st C	2nd C	3rd C	Last C
5	4	2	1

As long as the marks remain within each group then they are fair to all the students in these matched groups but look how distorted they become when the three classes are combined. Do not forget that the groups are matched for equal ability so the top of A group is the same level of ability as the top of B and of C.

Score		Overall position
10 marks	1st B	First
9 marks	2nd B	Second
8 marks		
7 marks	3rd B and 1st A	Joint third
6 marks	Last B and 2nd A	Joint fifth
5 marks	1st C	Seventh
4 marks	3rd A and 2nd C	Eighth
3 marks	Last A	Tenth
2 marks	3rd C	Eleventh
1 mark	Last C	Twelfth

Both nominal and ordinal scales have no numbers and they are scales which give rise to tests which are called *non-parametric* – no numbers.

Interval Scale

Interval scales have a set difference between scale points so it is possible to say that in an examination A achieved 75 per cent which was 10 per cent more than B who achieved 65 per cent. In all examinations the student's papers are given a raw mark scale where we can legitimately speak of differences between scale points. In education and training this is when candidates, learners and students are given marks; scores and percentages are awarded for work. There are pass marks and levels to gain credits and distinction: all the grades in national examinations and classes of degree are worked out on the interval scale.

When I was teaching in a small town in India there was a bit of a riot at the local university when the students demanded a lower pass rate from their local state governor. The dispute was most interesting because it had become almost an annual ritual, with the local government gaining some political popularity by bargaining for a 1 per cent cut that year and much better, as one of my Indian colleagues pointed out, than getting into the sorts of sex, drugs and drink problems that he had seen amongst English students at the same time. I asked my friendly colleague if the Indian examiners carried out the same number crunching on examination scores as UK examiners and he smiled and replied, 'Of course'.

When marks are awarded to any student work they are adjusted from the raw scores. For many years I helped to run a large examination under the regulations of the University of London which I still regard as a model traditional examination system. Here is an example of the processes I carried out after initial marking and marking moderation.

First, the individual questions were marked out of a maximum of 20 marks but the number of questions to be answered might vary, so my first job was to add up the full score for the exam, a total of 80 for a four-question exam, 100 for a five-question exam or 120 for a six-question exam, and turn this into a percentage, ie marks out of 100.

The next job was to draw up a 'tally' chart of the percentages to find out the overall distribution. I took a large piece of paper and wrote down the numbers 100 to 0 in descending order on the left-hand side of the sheet and tally-marked in each student's percentage score. I am not certain if it is true but I was told that the tally system was started by men counting the loading of articles onto a ship. As the first is carried by, you draw one short vertical line, then a second, then a third, then a fourth but as the fifth goes by you draw a diagonal line through the first four marks so you end up with easy to count totals made up of bundles of five. The tally chart in Figure 5.1 shows a typical bulge of distribution, with few students scoring high or low marks but the majority clustering around the middle of the distribution.

Down the right-hand side of my large sheet of paper I had three columns. In the first I put in the number of students who had scored that particular percentage of marks; this was easy addition from the tally-mark clusters. In the next column, starting at the top at 100 per cent, I drew up a running total; this started off with small numbers but added up to larger and larger numbers of students until I reached a grand total of all those sitting the examination at the bottom of the column.

Before I describe what went into the third column on the far outside right of my paper, I have to explain the traditional grading system. Examiners have a policy which is decided before any examination and is set on the percentages of students who will get the grades which are to be issued. They also decide the pass mark, the level at which a student will gain a credit or a distinction and so on. Here is a simple distribution of grades curve:

A	10 per cent
B	20 per cent
C	40 per cent
D	20 per cent
E	10 per cent

The examiners might decide that everyone who gained an A would be awarded a distinction, everyone given a B gained a credit and everyone given a C had passed. In this case everyone who had a D or an E might have failed, but the examiners could tell the D people that they were a 'marginal fail'. The system can be much more detailed by having A plus, A and A minus groups all the way through from A plus to E minus; that is decided by the examiners. The pass mark is also interesting: if the examiners want a few to succeed, the percentage mark required to pass is raised so high that few can achieve it; if the examiners want almost everyone to pass then the percentage is adjusted accordingly. The important thing for the poor victim of grading to remember is that all interval scales are quite arbitrarily decided by examiners and they are not an absolute D minus or even A plus on the actual person.

Now I will describe what I did in the third column. The grade plan was standard and had been decided long before my particular examination had taken place – a policy decision. I took the total number of people who had sat the examination together with the grade bands laid down on the plan and worked out the number of people who would fall into each band group. Take the simple distribution given above for 430 students sitting the examination:

A	10 per cent	43 people get an A
B	20 per cent	86 people get a B
C	40 per cent	172 people get a C
D	20 per cent	86 people get a D
E	10 per cent	43 people get an E

Once I had sorted out the number of people who could be allowed into each band group, I could look at the running total in column 2 and write in the cut-off points for each grade in column 3. This process allowed me to say for each examination:

Every student scoring over 86 per cent gets an A
Every student scoring between 72 and 85 per cent gets a B
Every student scoring between 57 and 71 per cent gets a C
Every student scoring between 38 and 56 per cent gets a D
Every student scoring less than 37 per cent gets an E.

In this examination the pass mark turns out to be 57 per cent but the actual percentage will vary each time because it depends on the performance of people sitting the examination. The examiners may decide that the quality of the candidates is rather low and they can decide to lower the percentage passing the exam by shifting the grade plan.

Ratio scales

A ratio scale is one which has a true zero point. This point must be a true zero, and not an arbitrary one such as zero degrees Fahrenheit when absolute zero temperature is defined as near minus 270 degrees Kelvin. Examples of ratio scales are the common physical ones of length, volume, time and so on. With these scales we not only have the properties of the preceding scales, but can also speak about ratios. We can say that ten seconds is twice as long as five seconds, that 100 pounds is one third as heavy as 300 pounds and so on.

There are very few attempts to create absolute scales in education and training and this is why Cronbach (1984) is so unusual.

DESCRIPTIVE STATISTICAL TECHNIQUES

Graphical presentation

One of the main purposes of descriptive statistics is to arrange raw data into a form which is easier to understand. Let us use a simple example; here are the marks for a single question on an examination paper which was scored out of 20 marks:

```
10 11  4 19 13  7 17 10  9  3  8  9 10 14 18 17  6  7
13 10  9 10  2 19 10  8  7  9 12 16 10  8  9  7 11 12
 9 10  4 16 11 10 12  5  9  8 17 18  9  7  8 11 12 10
19  6  4 10 11 12 10  9  8  6 13 14 10 15 10  9 11 10
 9 14 11  4 15 12 11  8  7 17  6 14  5 11 10  9 13  8
10 15  3 11 16 10  8  9 10 12
```

This data can be sorted into a tally-chart; see Figure 5.1.

		Total no.	Running total
20		0	
19	///	3	3
18	//	2	5
17	////	4	9
16	///	3	12
15	///	3	15
14	////	4	19
13	////	4	23
12	### //	7	30
11	### ###	10	40
10	### ### ### ////	19	59
9	### ### ///	13	72
8	### ////	9	81
7	### /	6	87
6	////	4	91
5	//	2	93
4	////	4	97
3	//	2	99
2	/	1	100
1		0	

Total: 100 students

Figure 5.1 *A tally-chart*

This data can be drawn into a frequency diagram like the one shown in Figure 5.2.

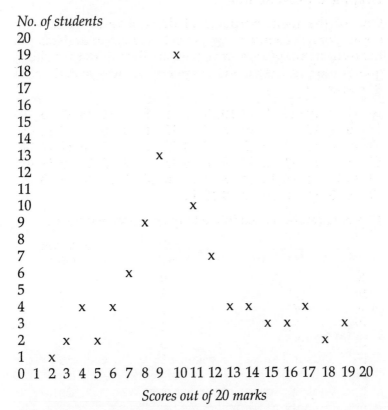

Figure 5.2 *Distribution of marks against number of students*

In practice this data can be condensed in two ways;

– by condensing the data into intervals so that it can be presented diagrammatically as a histogram or a bar chart
– by turning the raw scores into standard scores which will fit into a standard distribution curve.

Intervals

This information can be put into categories or intervals of data to make the large number of scores easier to handle. Some details of the data are lost in this process but the overall picture is easier to handle. With marks out of 20 for 100 candidates, let us form categories:

scoring over 16	9 students
scoring between 13 and 16	14 students
scoring between 9 and 12	49 students
scoring between 5 and 8	21 students
scoring under 5	7 students

This information can be displayed in a bar chart or histogram as shown in Figure 5.3.

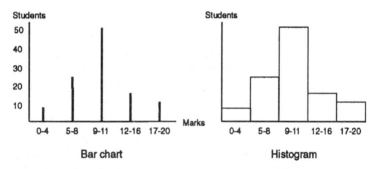

Figure 5.3 *Displaying the categories of students' marks*

Standard scores

This is a useful measure because it gives each person a clearer picture of where his or her marks stand in relation to the whole group of other learners who are sitting the same examination. We will come back to standard scores in a few pages but we need to cover some more ideas in descriptive statistics before the example can be progressed. Writing about statistics presents the problem of what to cover first, so you need to put a bookmark in here while I cover a few more basic ideas and then I can come back to this point. (Please note that there are advantages in the written form: in a live performance I would have great difficulty in saying 'put your thumb in here'!)

Central tendency

Surprisingly there are three ways in which the centre of a group can be measured and each method has its own uses. Let us start with the one which is most familiar.

The arithmetic mean

This is the most common measure of central tendency and what is generally meant by the word 'average'. You add up all the scores and divide by the number of people taking part and that gives you the average. Let us use our data example shown on page 78 and calculate the 'average'. Added together the marks make a total of 1035, so divided by 100 students this makes an average of 10 marks on the question.

The mode

You will have noticed that I have used the term 'central tendency' to head this section. Sometimes the plain arithmetical mean or average is not very useful for statistical purposes because by averaging out the numbers, the variations in the scores are lost. Suppose that you run a shoe shop in which most women customers buy size 4 and most men buy size 8. The arithmetic mean of shoe size would be size 6 but if you ordered a large number of size 6 shoes you would not be able to sell many pairs because they would be too small for most men and too large for most women. When you are selling shoes, you need to know which size is most often sold, and in the example I have given you have two sizes which have peak sales: size 4 for women and size 8 for men. My example of the shoes translated into statistical language would be written as:

> There are two separate *populations*: men and women. The *mode*, the most frequently occurring value, for women's shoe size is 4 and the *mode* for men's shoe size is 8.

When a frequency graph is drawn it is called a *distribution*. Figure 5.4 represents the frequency of sales against the shoe size. The twin peaks of sales are clearly shown and this is a tell-tale sign that there is not one but two populations combined in the graph: Figure 5.4 is a 'bimodal distribution'. Each population has a clear mode and there is a valley between the two where larger women's sizes and smaller men's sizes combine in numbers. The curves for women and men have been dotted in to show this overlap.

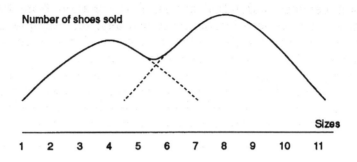

Figure 5.4 *A bi-modal distribution showing sales of shoes*

The median

Sometimes a set of measurements may contain one or two very untypical results which distort the arithmetical mean. This is where the 'median', the value of the middlemost score when the data are arranged in numerical order, comes in very useful. Suppose the shoe shop sold five pairs of shoes, in sizes 5, 8, 3, 7 and 15 (very big feet!). These sizes arranged in numerical order are 3, 5, 7, 8, 15 and the middle size is 7 and called the 'median'. Suppose that there were an even number of pairs of shoes sold, sizes 5, 8, 3, 7, 15 and 4. Rearranging them as 3, 4, 5, 7, 8, 15, there is no middle score so the two middle sizes 5 and 7 are taken as the median.

Range

The range is measured between the lowest to the highest value. This is a common measure and is used everyday; for instance, the price of a sandwich ranges from £1.19 to £1.99.

Types of data

Numerical data generally come in two kinds: measurement data when there is one score for each person in a group, and frequency data which is the number of times the same thing occurs.

Standard deviation

Sometimes there is very little difference in scores for any one test; all scores are close to the average. Other times there is a great difference in score values with a great variation between individual scores. This variation from the mean can be very important statistically; for example, in almost all tests which involve some physical task there is a marked difference between men's scores and women's scores. The scores for women seem to be clustered fairly closely round the mean, but men's scores always seem to have a much greater spread – the fastest but also the slowest. This statistical observation has wide implications.

⇨ **STOP AND REFLECT** ⇦

Women can have babies from the age of 11 until, say, their mid-40s, but some men can conceive children until they are in their 80s. Think about other statistics you have known which cover both men's and women's scores. Have you noticed that women's scores tend to cluster round the norm when men's score have a greater range, including the highest and the lowest?

Do you think that statistics which have an obvious biological basis transfer to all predictions? This would mean that when women have less variations in physical scores they are disadvantaged in predictions of cognitive or moral variations. I think this is the basis of much prejudice against women; what do you think?

All measures of central tendency ignore the range of scores and differences from the mean. The score which shows how far an individual score is from the central value is called the 'individual deviation'. This measure makes use of a simple arithmetical rule: when two negative numbers are multiplied together they make a positive number; for instance:

$$-2 \times -2 = 4$$

When you find an average by adding up numbers which are less than the average to numbers which are above average, all the differences cancel out, but when the differences are squared to make positive numbers then the variations from the mean can be calculated. It is probably easier in numbers than in words so here is an example.

This is a list of scores: 2, 5, 9, 10, 15, 19
First find the average:
$2 + 5 + 9 + 10 + 15 + 19 = 60$ $60 \div 6 = 10$

Score	Score - mean	Difference from mean	Squared difference
2	2 – 10	– 8	64
5	5 – 10	– 5	25
9	9 – 10	– 1	1
10	10 – 10	0	0
15	15 – 10	5	25
19	19 – 10	9	81
		Total 0	Total 196

By squaring the difference from the mean there is a measure of the variation of scores. The standard deviation is not as simple as finding the average. The sum of squares, in this case 196, is divided by the number of degrees of freedom, the total number of scores minus one, and then taking the square root. There are sound reasons for this rather complex calculation but unless you want to study the topic further, all you need to grasp is the way the standard deviation can be calculated to give a measure of how individual scores vary from the average. Here is the calculation of standard deviation for the example:

Sum of squares   196
Number of scores   6
Degrees of freedom   5 $196 \div 5 = 39.2$
The square root of 39.2 = 6.26
So the standard deviation (SD) = 6.26 and the general formula is:

$$SD = \frac{\text{sum of squares of individual differences from mean}}{\text{degrees of freedom}}$$

INFERENTIAL STATISTICAL TECHNIQUES

Variables

David Howell (1982) offers this definition

> properties of objects or events which can take on different values are referred to as variables. Hair colour, for example, is a variable because it is the property of an object (hair) and it can take on different values (brown, yellow, red, etc). Properties such as height, length and speed are variables for the same reason. We can further discriminate between DISCRETE VARIABLES (such as sex, marital status, and the number of heads in five flips of a coin) in which the variable can only take on one of a relatively few possible values, and CONTINUOUS VARIABLES (such as speed, time, and so on) where the variable could assume, at least in theory, any value between the lowest and the highest points on the scale.

This definition of a variable is extended in evaluation studies to *independent variables*, like learning strategies, which can be controlled by teachers, trainers and managers, and *dependent variables*, like the marks a learner scores on tests after experiencing different learning strategies, which are not under direct control. This may seem a difficult distinction so here is an activity.

=========== **ACTIVITY** ===========

Pick out the difference between independent and dependent variables.
Class size, examination marks, open learning, unit completion, competency-based programme, employment statistics.

This is a rather simple activity because it is easy to spot that class size, open learning and competency-based programmes are all variables which can be manipulated, whereas examination marks, unit completion and employment statistics are the quantitative dependent variables.

Populations and samples

A population can be defined as an entire collection, all the people or all the events; in the shoe selling exercise this would have been the entire number of men and women who could have come into the shop and in theory this would be all men and all women who come, for whatever reason, into the vicinity of the shop. On the other hand, the population might be quite small, like the left-handed women working on a factory production line. In cases involving small numbers, measurements can be taken from the entire population, but when the population is large and in some cases so large that it is uncountable, samples have to be taken for assessment or evaluation.

Deliberately or otherwise it is very easy to introduce bias when sampling. When this happens the sample will not represent the entire population and so it is important to take *random samples* – every element of the population has an equal chance of being included in the sample.

ACTIVITY

Taking a random sample.

In much assessment and evaluation, a 10 per cent sample is required and the best way to take a randomly selected sample is to find a general list, like the alphabetical list of all candidates taking a particular programme. Once you have such a list, choose a number between 0 and 9 – say 3 – and then select the 3rd, 13th, 23rd, 33rd and so on. This is a reliable method and once decided on, the selection *must not be altered* or bias will creep in. Tutors or trainers in an internal moderation exercise, for example, *must not substitute* with other candidates' work or the random sample is ruined. Find a suitable general list in your work and take a trial random 10 per cent sample.

Inference

Inferential statistics techniques use standard tests to:

- make sure that samples are truly random so that information collected for the sample can be applied to the whole population
- find out if an individual result varies significantly or very significantly from the mean
- compare the effect of a number of methods or to compare different markers (independent variables) and see if the effects (dependent variables) are significantly different
- see if there is a correlation between two independent variables.

Without some logical method of tackling data, assessment and evaluation would be unreliable.

RECORDING

The keeping of records forms an important basis for all statistics and teachers and trainers will find this task is usually carried out on a computer these days. You may need to set up a computer database to keep all the records you need. Small numbers of records can be kept in a paper-filing system, but whether you have your records on disk or in a filing cabinet, it is important that these records are secure and that confidentiality is maintained. One of the effects of the change to competency-based programmes and continuous assessment is that student information is now kept in busy college premises and at the workplace. Remember that it is an important basic teaching principle that 'respect for persons' is scrupulously observed at all times and the confidentiality of individual records is essential.

⇨ **STOP AND REFLECT** ⇦

Have you considered the 'power' that a teacher has when someone agrees to be a student?

Can you think of cases where you feel that one of your teachers abused this power?

Would you like your personal reports left lying around someone else's office?

A typical record of candidate's progress includes:

Name of candidate
Placement address, telephone number and contact person
Date of initial briefing
Dates of tutorial meetings and telephone calls
Action plans
Witness' statement of competence
Workshop reports, if needed
Witness statements on performance when required
Date of submission of portfolio evidence

================ **ACTIVITY** ================

Designing a record card.
Design a record card to summarize a candidate's progress over the whole period of your tutorial care.
Design a record card for action planning and review.

Chapter 6

Reliability and Validity

 CONCEPTS

Perfect assessment
Reliability
Validity
A reliable assessment system
Reliable assessors
Being fair to the candidate

PERFECT ASSESSMENT

Assessment has the general purpose of describing a person's level of achievement or potential and *evaluation* aims to describe the effectiveness of educational and training procedures. The tests or techniques used in both must summarize accurately these general aims. The best assessment of a person would be a complete life history: analysis without bias or distortion of examination results, achievement records, personal reports or standard test data, merely gives limited glimpses of the whole picture. In a perfect assessment the assessor achieves a flawless appraisal of exactly the quality which is under examination without disturbing the candidate.

It is impossible to achieve a perfect assessment in practice but there are guidelines which can be used to try to make assessment as fair and unbiased as possible. There are some good models for the construction of unbiased assessment systems; a structured system for interviewing is an example. This technique probably come closest to creating a fair system for general assessment of individual people. The system creates a very flexible framework for personnel selection for employment or learning programmes. Figure 6.1 shows the way in which an interview system can be built up.

Scores

Characteristic	Poor 1 2 3 4	Weak 5 6 7 8	Average 9 10 11 12	Good 13 14 15 16	Excellent 17 18 19 20
General education					
Specialist education					
Physical fitness					
Physical appearance					
Interpersonal skills					
Attitude					
Motivation					
Personality					
Leadership					
Etc					

Figure 6.1 *The start of a structured system*

All possible characteristics which are relevant to the selection process are listed down the left-hand side of the grid. The scoring system is worked out in five bands across the table on a scale of 1 to 20. The bands represent the range of measurement for each characteristic. All possible methods of assessment can be used and all possible human characteristics can be assessed in this system if they are relevant to the task in hand. This means that every assessment tool can be chosen if it is thought to be appropriate for the candidates and the aim of the interview. The grading between 1 and 20 might depend on formal qualifications and grades or an attitudinal test. The scale may be created as a measure of observed skilled performance or peer group assessment.

An interesting technique which can be built into the system is the 'band of acceptability'. One common mistake in interviewing is to look for the applicant with the best in every quality; this may lead to the selection of a person who is over-qualified for the job. Such a person might be discontent with the challenge of the work and look for the first opportunity to move on. It is quite possible to draw in both the minimum and the maximum levels of acceptability for every characteristic and so create a band of acceptability.

There is a principle which underlies structured interviewing which is central for all assessors: if it is important that the candidate possesses a human attribute then a way must be found to assess it. Some jobs, like psychiatric nursing, require humour, empathy or the lack of aggression; a method of assessing them at interview has to be found. It is unfair on applicants to be vague about the qualities which are required.

ACTIVITY

Creating an interview schedule.

The one thing about this system of interviewing is that it focuses the whole selection process, from application form to decision making after final interview. If you have to interview on a regular basis you might analyse the characteristics you want to assess and use this book for assessment techniques which can be applied for each of the selected qualities or achievements. Work out the bands of scale so that a final decision about the band of acceptability can be made. Remember that the system can use any suitable assessment method and choose any human attribute, provided that the applicants' rights are respected and individual freedom is not infringed.

Once, in the search for perfect assessment, I abandoned all systems which included another person asking questions because I felt that the candidate can find other people's questions irrelevant. You may have experienced questioning which seems trivial to your interests and needs, and understand my feeling that the candidate is probably the best person to ask relevant questions. This hypothesis cuts down available assessment methods quite drastically. I was left with a choice between introspection and George Kelly's (1955) personal construct theory. Kelly's theory has been developed into a grid method of assessment which is widely used in personal assessment, social psychology, cognition and psychotherapy (see Fransella and Bannister, 1977). This grid method has the unique advantage of setting a framework for investigation but leaving the choice of words and ideas to the candidate. I am sure that the results of my research reflected faithfully the real, personal thoughts of the people in my investigation but the main difficulty was translating this genuine information into any form of report. Accurate information has to be passed on to others without distortion for perfect assessment.

RELIABILITY

When I took my Masters degree in human learning and assessment, the buzz word was 'generalizability'. Any assessment can only take a small snapshot of human performance under limited circumstances and so great importance is placed on how much evidence can be relied on as a true indication of normal behaviour or performance. The question which bothered my lecturers was the extent to which it was possible to generalize from any one set of assessments. This idea of generalizability covered the assessment principles of reliability and validity but it was stressed that you can only generalize if assessment is both reliable *and* valid.

Defining reliability is difficult; I know of no definition which is entirely satisfactory. Here is one which is not tied to objective, quantifiable tests:

– a method of assessment is reliable when individuals, having the same ability, knowledge or skill, achieve the same score or result whenever the method is used and whoever is being assessed.

Reliable measures provide consistent and unambiguous information and reduce chance and random conditions. Factors which improve reliability include:planned situations, unbiased and trained assessors and prepared students.

VALIDITY

A good definition of validity is another which is hard to find. Here is my attempt:

– a method of assessment is said to be valid if it measures the intended aims, goals, objectives, performance or quality.

Focusing on the *intended* quality and not straying sideways into unintentional assessment is the essence of validity. For example, when the intention is to assess a knowledge of chemistry, marks should not be assigned to essay-writing skills, unless it is intended to assess the ability to express chemical ideas in a written report.

There are several ways in which validity can be achieved; below I will discuss the factors and try to show different applications of each principle.

Face validity

This is important for the motivation of the candidate: assessment must be seen to be relevant. Mechanical engineers expect tests to assess mechanical engineering examples and catering students expect problems which are set in catering situations. The underpinning science principles may be the same in both cases but an engineer expects Newton's Laws of Motion to be behind problems within mechanical settings, and a caterer expects questions involving Ohm's law to be set in a kitchen.

Empirical validity

The assessment must be able to be carried out in practice; within the economic resources of the candidate and the institution. Assessors must be careful to use equipment, materials and human resources which are freely available. It is not a valid test if few people can afford the cost.

Construct validity

Written examinations are a poor method of measuring a health professional's empathy with patients. Construct validity is assured when observation at work, peer reports or self-assessment methods are used.

Concurrent validity

The assessor has to identify the trait which needs to be assessed so that the correct assessment tool can be chosen.

Many years ago I attended a fascinating day of assessment which was put on by a gas company for their top salesmen. The object of the day was to identify the qualities of a good gas salesmen and how these qualities could be assessed at an interview. The experiment was quite simple. Over 100 top salesmen were placed in an examination hall and given every standard test that the company could find. As soon as the tests were completed they were marked to see if everyone scored highly, or even poorly on the same test. It was a tremendous effort and some very surprising results started to emerge: top salesmen ranged from highly intelligent to rather stupid; top salesmen could be highly extrovert or quite introvert; no general personality trait seemed to correlate and then, quite late in the day, an odd little test scored highly for all the men in the room. It was an interpersonal skills test on the sequences in which other people are approached. I forget the origin of the test but I think it had something to do with audience participation for actors. Basically all the salesmen selected the sequence:

You   We   I

There were lots of examples but they all followed the general pattern. '*You* have a problem, *we* can tackle it together and *I* will do . . .'. Confirmation of the usefulness of this test came from an odd source. Some years later my husband went on an expensive sales training course and the motto was, 'You, We, I'. I am still not sure what you would call this trait which was effectively identified for concurrent validity.

⇨ **STOP AND REFLECT** ⇦

When you ask a question does it seem relevant to the learner?

Do you pay regard to the economic cost of testing?

How can you be sure that the assessment tool you use measures the quality you want to assess?

Are you sure that you have identified the quality for assessment correctly?

A RELIABLE ASSESSMENT SYSTEM

Timetables for assessment

The candidate must not be tired and fatigued unless the test is specifically designed as a test of human endurance. Many training programmes have a punishing assessment schedule at the end. When I was taking some final examinations I had two days of examinations with two three-hour examinations each day: the end of the third examination and the whole of the fourth examination assessed resistance to tiredness and fatigue more than knowledge; as I was not on an endurance programme, this was unreliable assessment.

There should be advanced notice of dates and times for assessment.

Arrangements for assessment must be clear to the candidate

The location must be suitable for the method of assessment, with tidy and safe working areas prepared before a practical, and quiet, spacious and well-aired examination rooms for written tests.

There should be clear definitions of what is to be assessed together with details of the assessment methods. A lack of clarity can cause unreliability in both norm-referenced and criterion-referenced testing.

Candidates should have clear and unambiguous instructions for the assessment method, with no trick questions. It is important that all instructions, like the rubric on an examination paper, are written in terms which the candidate understands. Old examination hands will advise candidates to 'Read the paper', and this is good advice for everyone facing assessment. However, there is a responsibility on assessors to write very clear instructions because most learners suffer from some form of test anxiety which makes it more difficult to apply common sense in stressful conditions.

When I was sitting my examination for a Masters level in human learning and assessment I was delighted to find an error in the examination paper. One question contained a section which formed the whole of another question. Instead of answering four whole questions chosen from the 11 or so available, I answered three and a half questions but wrote a claim on the examination paper for the missing half and asked the marker to re-mark one of my full questions as the answer to the overlap question. As one of the questions covered reliability and internal verification, I felt fairly confident that I could get away with such cheek. Some weeks later when I received some good results I was greeted with sheepish grins from my tutors and we all had a good laugh.

Well-ordered assessment procedures and records

Mistakes can be made in recording and the 'number crunching' part of assessment. Simple clerical errors can occur when the candidate misreads the lines of an answer sheet. I have seen one candidate's responses which were a line out on every item. I wondered at the time if the student suffered from astigmatism. Markers can err in the totalling of marks on a paper and the transposing of successful achievement from one list to another. With records on computers there is the added danger of errors in keying in data.

Systems are the responsibility of internal and external verifiers (see Chapters 7 and 8).

Running a formal examination

Reliability may depend on the way in which the examination is run. I believe that the quality of an educational institution can be judged by clean boards, straight overhead transparency projection and the attention to detail in running examinations. Here are some notes on the almost lost art of running examinations:

- Make certain that the examination papers are prepared so that the questions cover the syllabus evenly, are written in clear English with unambiguous instructions and are relevant to the candidates.
- Watch the secrecy of the papers at the time of writing, printing and storage before the examination. Pay especial attention to access to examination papers on computers.
- Order and maintain stocks of all examination materials such as answer booklets, supplementary paper, blotting paper if necessary, tables which may be required, stationery which may be used for the return of results and even string if it is required to tie the examination papers together. There may be special answer sheets for computer-marked answer papers.
- Keep special watch on examination materials, because an easy way for a candidate to cheat is to carry a sheet of answer paper into the examination. It is very bad practice not to clear all spare paper at the end of an examination.

- Arrange the booking of the examination room and check that you have enough room to place examination desks at proper spacing. Five feet all round is a reasonable distance between desks. Arrange with caretakers that special examination desks and chairs are set out in the room. Check if you need to make provision for people with disabilities, such as wheelchair access.

- Check that all candidates have an examination number and that notices of these numbers and the rooms in which candidates will be sitting are displayed at least three weeks before the examination. Ask the candidates to check their examination number; this will insure that anyone who has been missed can be fitted in. At the same time, post up examination regulations and sample papers so that the candidates know what the format of the examination will be.

- Arrange for pre-examination materials to be made available for the candidates if necessary.

- Print the examination numbers or write out cards for each candidate so that the cards can be fixed to the desks.

- Arrange an invigilation list and give your invigilators time to check for substitutes if necessary. Write a schedule for the laying out of the examination materials in the rooms before the examination, the labelling of desks and the collection of examination papers from a central safe point. Write a list of duties for invigilators, including procedures for entering and leaving the exam room, absence from the examination room during the examination, relief for invigilators, and the collection of examination papers and materials at the end of the examination, with return to a secure place. You will need to issue your invigilators a reminder just before the examination.

- Have 'Silence, examination in progress' notices printed and make sure that these notices are put up immediately before the examination and taken down immediately afterwards.

- Deal with domestic duties such as the provision of water for the examination room.

- Now deal with the medical problems. It is amazing how students who have been healthy all year produce a raft of illnesses when examination time comes round. The secret is to make every arrangement possible to get them to attend the actual examination. I have put up drawing boards so that students with bad backs can stand to write out their answers. I have placed students at the door nearest the lavatory. I have put out soft chairs and stools for expectant mums. I have put hayfever sufferers in ante-rooms so that they can sneeze in peace. Care and attention beforehand can mean that students perform to their best in the event.

- People with physical barriers need even greater planning. Candidates with visual impairment are well supported in the UK: examination papers can be written in Braille and most boards will accept an amanuensis. Such assistance can also be available for people who cannot write – for example, because of a broken wrist or some such injury. Some visually impaired candidates can use a special typewriter with large print and for these candidates I used to arrange for the examination paper to be read at dictation pace before the start of the examination and again used adjacent rooms so that the noise did not disturb other candidates. Many people with physical barriers may need extra time which is usually granted but it is important not to overrun for too long or the examination become a trial of endurance.

- The examination rooms should be well cleaned, neatly set out and well ventilated. Candidates often sweat with anxiety and a poorly ventilated room can become quite noxious on a hot day. Uncomfortable physical conditions may affect the reliability of the examination.

- When the desks have been laid out and labelled, a plan should be drawn which indicates the position and numbers of candidates. This plan has three purposes: it helps candidates find their alloted place; it is easy to check which candidates were absent from an examination while the examination is in progress; and it is possible, after the event, to check physical proximity in an examination room if a candidate is suspected of copying.

One invigilator is in charge of each examination room and has the responsibility for making a report which includes the plan and absentees as well as any incidents which may have taken place.

ACTIVITY

Reliable written tests.
I have just described the full procedure for running formal examinations but the same general rules apply to any written test wherever it takes place. Check the procedures for any testing which is under your control to make sure that you are using reliable procedures.

RELIABLE ASSESSORS

Competency-based assessment is used in many countries for vocational, technical and professional training. In the UK National Standards have been developed by the Training Development Lead Body (TDLB). These TDLB units, which are divided into three or four elements, provide guidelines for assessors. The TDLB jargon can be difficult to understand but the ideas are useful. I will give the element titles for two units and explain how each element ensures reliable assessor practice.

D321 Agree and review a plan for assessing performance
This element is designed to ensure that every candidate is given equal access to fair assessment. The assessor is expected to discuss the method of assessment and the gathering of evidence to make assessment decisions with the candidate. When an assessment plan is created on a personal basis, the assessor is able to take into account individual needs and cut out unfair discrimination.

D322 Collect and judge performance evidence against criteria
The assessor must be as unobtrusive as possible when observation takes place, to avoid affecting the candidate's

performance. Direct observation does ensure that all assessment is of the candidate's own work. The assessor can use a checklist to make sure that only the relevant criteria are assessed.

D323 Collect and judge knowledge evidence
It is not possible to judge understanding of a practical performance without asking questions. Oral and written questions can be used to assess understanding but the assessor must have knowledge of the particular subject matter so that the questions have face validity for the candidate. If a witness is being used to observe a performance then the assessor needs to know the qualifications of the witness to make sure that the observer knew the relevant subject matter. Because the assessor or witness can speak directly to the candidate, problems of reliability which may arise from a candidate's inexperience of assessment or special assessment needs can be dealt with at this stage.

D324 Make assessment decisions and provide feedback
The assessor has direct contact with the candidate so that there can be no delay or ambiguity in providing feedback on the assessment decision. The candidate has the advantage of being able to ask the assessor directly if any misunderstanding of the assessment method or decision has occurred. The assessor is required to show that results have been accurately placed into the recording system.

D331 Agree and review an assessment plan
The first element in the D33 unit includes the assessment plan for observing a performance which was covered in D321 and moves into the reliability and validity of other assessment methods such as simulations, projects and assignments, questioning, candidate and peer reports, candidates' prior achievement and learning. The assessor must show an understanding of a wide range of ways of making assessment decisions but the same principles of consultation and planning with the candidate apply.

D332 Judge evidence and provide feedback
The assessor has to show skill in judging the authenticity, sufficiency and reliability of evidence which has been provided by other people or by methods which do not involve direct observation. It is important that the assessor has a knowledge of assessment theory, rather than an understanding of the candidate's subject matter which was so important in D323.

D333 Make assessment decisions using differing sources of evidence and provide feedback
The assessor has to provide feedback to the candidate, like in D324, but the main emphasis is on satisfying the internal verifier that the assessment decisions met all the quality control requirements of the verification process. Assessors are the front-line workers in a whole assessment industry which runs from shop-floor and small examination room testing to national institutions. This element is a vital link in the chain of quality assurance which guarantees the reliability and validity of the whole certification and assessment process.

Careless marking will always cause unreliability and I have already given some examples on page 35. However, it is worth remembering that assessment systems do tend to overload teachers and trainers. A good example of marking without thinking occurred when I asked a colleague to check over my marking of a student's assignment after I had attended one of his lectures. Unfortunately I handed to him not only the student's work but my own notes on his lecture as well. The student got 7 out of 10 and my notes on his lecture got 8 out of 10.

BEING FAIR TO THE CANDIDATE

There is a long tradition of using assessment at the end of training as a 'right of entry'. Historical accounts are dotted with horror stories about apprentice boys being built into barrels at the end of their training or forced to climb soot-covered chimneys as part of an initiation ceremony. These rites seem to be used by some trainers to distinguish between 'real training' and that soft option, 'education'. Special entry tests are one way in which barriers are artificially raised before a new person is allowed to join a select working elite. The days of 'crossing the line' ceremonies are long gone and there should be no divide between assessment in education and assessment in training. If a quality, like the ability to withstand pain or show bravery in the face of unreason, is required for a profession or trade, then this quality must be written into the assessment plan.

In fair assessment the candidate is not bored. When achievement motivation is discussed, it is clear that people with confidence and a grasp of the subject matter become bored and careless if asked to carry out tedious examinations and tests. It is possible to assess most subjects by multiple-choice items provided that you write enough of them, but the test quickly becomes unreliable because the candidates become bored.

Candidates must be motivated. Examiners and testers tend to assume that candidates will put their best foot forward but this is not necessarily the case. Assessment must be meaningful to the candidate. I am sure that lack of motivation may be a real cause of failing to do well in school examinations because it gives the pupil the excuse, 'I did not really try'.

Reliability in assessment requires training for the candidate. Most of us give candidates advice on preparation before the event:

- Remember that being assessed is rather like entering an athletic event. You need to be fit, relaxed, fed but not too well fed, and well slept.
- Pace your revision over the weeks before the assessment and use a reliable technique for remembering essential facts (see Book 1 of this series).
- Plan carefully beforehand so that you know exactly where you have to go, how long the journey will take and what you will need in the way of special clothing, tools, pens, instruments and personal documentation.
- Arrive in plenty of time but if you are feeling nervous, try some brisk exercise, like running up a few stairs: this will release tension. In my student days we used to dance La Bamba at the door of the exam room!

Here are a few notes on the pep-talk I give to my own students when they prepare to sit a formal essay-type examination:

- If you have not taken an examination for some time work out how long you will have for each question. For instance, four questions in three hours will give 40 to 45 minutes for each question; practise writing on one question for 40 minutes.
- Force yourself to read the examination paper carefully. It is a good idea to use a highlighter to pinpoint key words. Remember the experiment in which students were asked to choose four questions out of five for an examination and were then persuaded to stay on longer at the end to complete the fifth, rejected question. In no case did the fifth question score lowest marks – which is a very interesting result, but I would love to know how the examiners persuaded the candidates to stay on.
- Mark the questions you choose as your best, next best and others. Work out how long you have for each question and start with your second best. Stop writing the answer for the first question as soon as the time limit is up. Remember that you are never given more than maximum marks for a single question and it is much easier to gain marks by spending more time on your weaker areas. Tackle the other questions in the middle of the examination, making sure that you spend the allocated time for each question trying to improve what may be weaker answers. As soon as the time is ready to start your final question, turn to your first choice and run as hard as you can up to the final bell. The main reason for this sequence is to avoid spending half the exam time on your best subject area when you can never improve on full marks which may represent only 25 per cent of the total exam.
- When calculating the time for each question, try to leave a few minutes for re-reading answers so that you can spot the grosser mistakes.

Chapter 7

External Verification

 CONCEPTS

Societies, guilds and professional bodies
What is a university?
National Vocational Qualifications
Lead bodies
The work of an external verifier
Quality assurance

SOCIETIES, GUILDS AND PROFESSIONAL BODIES

Training and assessment used to be a family affair. The son
of a blacksmith was expected to become a blacksmith and a
thatcher's son a thatcher. This trade description is the
origin of many English surnames. In medieval times each
trade had a guild which controlled apprenticeship and
standards. The City and Guilds of London Institute (C and
G) has its origins in this ancient system and the Royal
Society of Arts (RSA) also has a long and distinguished
history. The examination sections of both the C and G and
the RSA were started after the Great Exhibition of 1851.

Craft training and assessment has developed from the
passing on of skills from parent to child in every country of

the world. Most assessment systems are influenced by universities and professional organizations which are the products of a society's history and political roots. It is impossible to lift an educational system from one country and transplant it in another. Teachers and trainers must be familiar with their own system and so for external and internal verification I must describe my own current situation in the UK. Readers from other countries will find clear parallels because all assessment systems are controlled by higher education, professional bodies and the government.

Many of the professional bodies of occupations such as surveyors, accountants and physiotherapists have Royal Charters and control over their professions by selected university awards or special examinations. The maintenance of standards and quality within each profession is very much the concern of the members of that profession.

Other awarding bodies, like BTEC, have come about by more recent legislation. I used to teach and examine an Ordinary National Certificate for science laboratory technicians. The ONCs started in the 1920s but they changed to a variety of qualifications under TEC (Technician Education Council), BEC (Business Education Council) and DATEC (Design and Art Technician Education Council). This flutter of separate awarding bodies came together again under the BTEC banner. The ONC scheme had a higher level, Higher National Certificate (HNC), and both schemes catered for part-time students. The full-time Diploma system, OND and HND, was introduced in the 1950s. Some HNDs became full degree equivalents when the Colleges of Advanced Technology, CATS, became new technological universities in 1974 but there are still remnants of the National Certificate and Diploma system today. HNDs certainly exist in engineering training and the scheme is the origin of the 'National' in the BTEC National awards. These changes did not affect some lecturers at all. I remember one chemistry lecturer taking down his ONC teaching files and changing the labels to TEC. Some years later when I visited the same staff room I noticed that these same files were relabelled BTEC and no doubt they are now called NVQ.

Verification has become something of a growth industry and although there are some respectable and sound organizations, I am not too happy about some of the newer expansions in the validation market. Quality control is expensive and it is not easy to maintain high standards when many organizations are working in the external verification market.

All these awarding bodies have clearly defined regulations for maintaining quality and standards. Here is the introduction to the 1995 Handbook for BTEC:

The role of the External Verifier and External Examiner

Introduction to the General Role
1.1 You are the formal representative of BTEC working in partnership with your centres to provide a regular and consistent review of BTEC provision. You help to ensure that those involved in planning, delivery, and assessment of qualifications:
- maintain the national standards of qualifications awarded by BTEC
- assess students' performance in accordance with published specifications
- have a clear commitment to ensuring and improving quality. ...

WHAT IS A UNIVERSITY?

In the UK, more and more training and assessment is being linked into the higher education system, so I will ask the question: what is a university? The first universities were created by Royal Charter. The king or queen gave the centre of learning the right to issue degrees and the control of the way in which degrees were awarded was left to the university itself. This is still true today: universities are autonomous and have a statutory right to issue their own degrees.

The universities can extend their degree awards by introducing external degrees. The system of external awards began when a college or specialist institution wanted wider recognition for its advanced courses and high level training; these centres of excellence applied to a nearby university to have advanced work recognized as an external degree of the university. The university set up an inspection and a quality control system which involved at least external examiners from the university to check the standard of work before any degree was awarded. To maintain the standards of the university, many of these external study routes were made noticeably more difficult than similar study within the university; some external degree candidates who studied part-time took several years to achieve qualification and their awards were a symbol of dedication and effort. By the 1960s the external degree system had become extensive and it was possible, for example, to take an external degree from the University of London as far away as Newcastle or Cardiff. In the Far East it was possible to take a degree from the University of Calcutta in most parts of South-east Asia.

The Open University, called at first the 'University of the Air', branched away from the traditional pattern and very much increased the access for students all over the UK. Although many of the teaching and organization methods are unique in their use of modern media, the fundamental structure of university autonomy remains. Students of the Open University do not attend a university campus for their studies but they do have summer schools for group study and there is an extensive system of local tutorials.

The creation of the Council for National Academic Awards, the CNAA, was an even greater step away from the traditional pattern of awarding degrees. The British government set up a degree awarding body which was a university without campus, courses, teaching or research. The CNAA was simply a system for approving and maintaining quality control of courses within institutions which wished to offer degrees. The CNAA approval was widely used by institutions formerly using external university degrees and, indeed, the introduction of the CNAA was largely motivated by the need to standardize the external degree system which had become extensive and within which it was difficult to assure quality standards.

The CNAA work has been largely superseded by the creation of a further wave of new universities from the polytechnic section. My own university was granted 'Power to Award Degrees under Section 76(2)(a) of the Further and Higher Education Act 1992'. The Privy Council, in exercising powers conferred by Section 77 of the Act, consented to the adoption of the name 'University of Greenwich' by the Polytechnic.

Quality control in a university

In theory the universities are responsible to no one for quality control but in practice quite severe standards can be applied. At present the British government imposes standards by holding the financial purse-strings in the form of the Higher Education Funding Committee. To qualify for government funding through the HEFC, the universities have to open up departments for inspection and the results are published in national newspapers which record which university departments are excellent, satisfactory or unsatisfactory.

Over time each university builds up a reputation on the strength of past performance and research so that career advisers will say, 'Oh, go to — for biochemistry, it is very sound, but you would do better to try for — if you want to study organic chemistry'.

⇨ **STOP AND REFLECT** ⇦

Many teacher and trainers give career advice to learners. How do you keep up to date with the available awards?

Can you be sure that programmes which used to be reliable are still good and up to date?

If you think you provide high quality training, how do you advertise the fact?

New universities, like mine, have to build their reputations, so very great care is taken to lay down mission statements, rules and regulations for all staff to follow. Here are some notes from regulations on quality control:

> The University will periodically examine its system for developing and sustaining academic quality, including the standards actually achieved by students, its approaches to teaching and learning and to research and scholarly activity in support of the curricula.

This evaluation aims to demonstrate accountability, academic leadership, staff and student contributions to academic policy and effective internal communications.

> The University will carry out a regular process of self-evaluation and audit, in order to discharge its responsibilities for the maintenance of academic quality and standards.

This audit covers review events, monitoring the student experience, the appointment of external examiners and the procedures for the confering of awards.

NATIONAL VOCATIONAL QUALIFICATIONS

In 1986 the British government carried out a review of vocational qualifications in England and Wales. The report of the working party recommended:

- a National Council for Vocational Qualifications (NCVQ) to regulate all vocational examinations
- a national framework of levels of achievement for all vocational qualifications.

The results of this decision have radically altered the nature of British vocational and general education. The NCVQ first tackled the criteria which would form the basis of the new structure and here are some of the important criteria.

Competency-based assessment

(All the quotations in the next sections are taken from the *NVQ Criteria and Guidance* (January 1995) published by the

Employment Department and The National Council for Vocational Qualifications.)

Competancy-based assessment was seen as 'a defined activity against pre-determined standards or criteria which might require intellectual, personal or practical achievements.' NVQ qualifications must:

- be based on national standards required for performance in employment
- relate to future needs with regards to technology, markets and employment patterns
- be based on learning by any mode – distance, coaching or APL
- be based on learning with no set time-scale – no courses
- be based on learning in any location – home, work, college
- have valid and reliable assessments ensuring that national standards can be achieved at work.

Relevance to work

(The NVQ system is closely linked with learning work skills, so the following factors are important.)

- task performance in context
- task management, ie, the skills to manage a group of tasks and prioritize between them
- contingency management, ie, the skills to recognize and deal with irregularities and variances in the immediate working environment
- role/environmental skills, ie, the skills to work with others and cope with environmental factors which are required to fulfil the wider role expectations
- the focus of assessment is therefore direct observation of a candidate's performance under normal operating conditions in the workplace

Knowledge and understanding

Assessment of knowledge should concentrate on:

- knowledge of the variation in circumstances that might be expected and how practices and procedures should be modified to meet different circumstances, over the range which is expected
- an understanding of the principles or theory which explain the nature of the function or activity to be assessed.

NVQ levels

All NVQs must be positioned in one of the following five levels of the framework:

Level 1: competence which involves the application of knowledge in the performance of a range of varied work activities, most of which may be routine or predictable.

Level 2: competence which involves the application of knowledge in significant range of varied work activities, performed in a variety of contexts. Some of the activities are complex or non-routine and there is some individual responsibility and autonomy. Collaboration with others, perhaps through membership of a work group or team, may often be a requirement.

Level 3: competence which involves the application of knowledge in a broad range of varied work activities performed in a wide variety of contexts, most of which are complex and non-routine. There is considerable responsibility and autonomy, and control or guidance of others is often required.

Level 4: competence which involves the application of knowledge in a broad range of complex technical or professional work activities performed in a wide variety of contexts and with a substantial degree of personal responsibility and autonomy. Responsibility for the work of others and the allocation of resources is often present.

Level 5: competence which involves the application of a significant range of fundamental principles across a wide and often unpredictable variety of contexts. Very substantial personal autonomy and often significant responsibility for the work of others and for the allocation of substantial resources feature strongly, as do personal accountabilities for analysis and diagnosis, design, planning, execution and evaluation.

NVQ design

The design of NVQs must ensure that there is:

- a clear structure which can be readily understood by all users
- a set of mandatory units which forms a major part of the qualification
- progress from one level to the next and to related areas of competence
- comparability between NVQs in similar occupational areas.

Mandatory units which form a major part of any NVQ contain the functions which give the occupation its fundamental character and provide a broad basis of competence for employment within the sector and adaptability for future progression

Optional units provide breadth yet flexibility in the structure of an NVQ. They must sustain breadth and be applicable to reasonable numbers of candidates, and avoid complex rules for combining or clustering units.

General NVQs (GNVQs) have been designed to bridge the academic/vocational divide. GNVQs, introduced in 1991, are intended to cover broad occupational areas, and offer opportunities to develop knowledge and understanding, and to gain appreciation of how to apply them at work. They also form an accepted route to higher education, with level 3 of comparable standard to A and AS level qualifications. Although they share the same structure as NVQs in terms of units, elements and performance criteria, there are also some important differences. GNVQs will not attest occupational or professional competence. They are to be based on 'statements of attainment' rather than 'statements of competence'. Also, GNVQs are to be designed so that they can be administered and assessed in educational institutions.

ACTIVITY

Explaining the NVQs.

One of the difficulties about any innovation in education and training is that each new initiative has to be explained over and over again to people entering a new field. NVQs are no exception; indeed, they seem to be particularly difficult to explain and understand. You might find it easy to read over the last section about NVQs and pick out the salient points so that you can write a precis in preparation for a time when you have to explain this new development.

LEAD BODIES

Once the NCVQ had decided the rules and criteria, they asked all sections of industry to form lead bodies to represent each occupational area. Some areas of industry got off to a good start because there were existing bodies, like the old Industrial Training Boards, which formed a basis for representing a particular interest.

Here are some more notes on the NCVQ criteria:

Lead bodies are responsible for defining, maintaining, and improving national standards of performance for NVQs. The Employment Department has overall responsibility for the structure of the lead bodies, and each lead body must have Employment Department recognition. Lead bodies should inform NCVQ of their plans to develop new standards or redevelop those existing.

Lead bodies represent their sector of employment, including small and leading-edge employers and must have credibility as employment-led organisations. Their composition, and the consultations which they undertake with their sectors, should ensure that the standards they detail are widely acceptable to employers and employees. They should also have access to advice which allows them to judge the accessibility of their standards. Lead bodies need to work with awarding bodies in the formation and structuring of NVQs.

Some working quickly and some rather more slowly, the lead bodies produced national standards of competency for their occupational area and agreed with the NCVQ which of the competences needed to be achieved at each NVQ level. It is now possible to state very accurately what a level 3 hairdresser is able to do and what a level 1 mechanical engineering craftsmen should have achieved.

There are some national standards which are in the unique position of crossing all occupational areas. Two main examples of universal standards are those for management and training. Each has its own performance criteria and its own underpinning knowledge but both can be applied to all the other occupational areas. The NCVQ encourages the use of management standards and they insist that all assessors in NVQ programmes should hold competency-based assessor awards as part of the quality control system. Until 1995 GNVQ assessors were expected to hold training assessor NVQ awards; special GNVQ assessor units have now been introduced.

Awarding bodies

It must be remembered that the NCVQ does not write national standards: that is the job of the lead bodies. Nor does the NCVQ run an assessment and verification process for NVQ awards: that is the business of the awarding bodies. Awarding bodies apply to the NCVQ for permission to run NVQ programmes; the situation is confused because many lead bodies also act as awarding bodies for their own subject area and related units, like management and training. With the need for continuous professional development, many professional organizations, and more recently the universities, are beginning to apply for permission to act as NVQ awarding bodies.

Here are some notes on the NCVQ criteria for awarding bodies; they must:

- collect and evaluate data arising from self-monitoring
- use procedures for the approval of centres
- select, train, coordinate and ensure the competence of external verifiers
- provide guidance and advice to existing and potential centres, assessors, verifiers and candidates
- administer candidate registration and certification
- administer and arrange financial links with the NCVQ
- market NVQs and units
- monitor the award.

'NVQ awarding bodies are accountable to NCVQ for the delivery of NVQs', so that they:

- recognize all relevant professional occupational groups
- demonstrate capability in the range of assessment required
- apply rigorous quality assurance mechanism
- liaise with national bodies
- 'undertake to provide feedback to inform the maintenance and development of the quality and relevance of the statement of competence, knowledge specification and evidence requirements to meet present and future needs'
- are responsible for the certification and administration of NVQs and regularly provide NCVQ with information on certificates achieved and centres approved
- operate the NVQ systems of credit accumulation and transfer by issuing certificates of unit credit, and recognizing certificates of unit credit issued by other awarding bodies

(the next few points are very important)
- 'have a written equal opportunities policy, a strategy for its implementation, a means of monitoring and acting upon its outcomes, and a means of communicating this to all those using the NVQ system'
- 'make the awards available to all those who are able to achieve the required standard, by whatever means, and free from barriers which restrict access and progression'
- 'be free from overt or covert discriminatory practices and pay due regard to the special assessment requirements of individuals who may require support to undertake assessment'
- 'be free from age or other restrictions unless legally required'
- 'publish an appeals systems to resolve any disputes arising out of assessment and verification centre approval procedures'.

THE WORK OF AN EXTERNAL VERIFIER

In all areas of training and education external moderators and examiners are appointed to have overall control of the quality of educational and training programmes. Here is a general list of their responsibilities:

- to judge impartially
- to compare an individual's performance with his or her peers
- to approve the form and content of examinations and other forms of assessment
- to agree changes in assessment procedures
- to attend examiners' meetings
- to see all students' work
- to overview marks given by internal verifiers
- to conduct a *viva voce* examination (usually used when a candidate has unavoidably missed an examination)
- to check that processes follow the assessment regulations
- to report on the effectiveness of the assessment methods.

External examiners have a great deal of power and it is important that they are experienced and responsible. I have only once taken part in the summary dismissal of an external examiner when, instead of observing a lesson to check that the student should receive a distinction in practical teaching, he picked a violent political argument with the student teacher in front of the class and failed him on the spot! This action created a few problems because external examiners, like judges, are nearly impossible to sack. External moderators are usually appointed by the awarding bodies.

An increasing number of assessors are becoming involved with NVQ external verification. Currently I am an NVQ external verifier for a university, two technical colleges, a large accredited training centre, two county training centres for St John Ambulance, a management centre, a County Council and three commercial training businesses. This shows the spread of the NVQ system in the UK today. The Training and Development Lead Body (TDLB) Unit D36 is designed for external verifiers and so I will give the title of each element and a short description of the theory of external verification in each case.

D351 Provide information, advisory and support services to centres
The external verifier is the link between the awarding body and the NVQ centre. He or she is expected to provide accurate, complete, current and relevant support on the following topics:

- planning, resourcing, quality assurance and recording arrangements in the centre
- the needs of candidates with special assessment requirements
- centre staff training and development for their assessment roles
- interpretations of the awarding body guidance and criteria
- national standards
- quality assurance arrangements

- equality of access and the elimination of unfair discrimination.

D352 Verify assessment practice and centre procedures
The external verifier helps the centre to establish and maintain a verification plan which covers the following principles:

- inspection of a representative sample of assessments
- effective use of resources in meeting awarding body verification requirements
- monitoring according to the awarding body requirements
- the quality and consistency of assessors' judgements
- positive feedback when good practice is identified
- prompt action if there is a departure from awarding body requirements
- checks that national standards are met
- checks that valid assessment is achieved
- disputes regarding assessment are resolved equitably.

D353 Maintain records of visits and provide feedback to awarding body
The external verifier has to make certain that the centre documentation is correct and accurate. This includes:

- verification records and the frequency and purpose of visits
- reports of centre visits and advisory activities
- reports to the awarding body
- recommendations for improvements to assessment practices.

Quality assurance is an increasing component of the NCVQ's own work. The NCVQ (or individuals or organizations working for the NCVQ) will require access to information held by awarding bodies for the purpose of quality assurance and control so that the information may be audited. The awarding body must facilitate access to such information, which will not be used for any purpose other than the quality audit and it is the external verifier who collects centre information to meet these requirements.

ACTIVITY

Taking an overview of your own verification processes.
The NCVQ has had to be very precise in the specification of quality assurance procedures. You may find it useful to be specific about the aims and objectives of your own verification process. Read through the NCVQ rules on external verification and compare this with your own practice.

QUALITY ASSURANCE

Training and educational qualifications fall into the general field of Total Quality Management. There are quality assurance systems which fit into national, international and European quality standards. You may find a system which suits your area of teaching or training interest. For example, British Standard 5750 (and its international equivalent, ISO 9000) raises a series of questions about quality assurance including:

- checking supplies and suppliers
- policy aims and objectives
- organization, structures and processes essential for management
- contract drafting
- functions of design and development
- documentation
- resource management.

The list extends to every operation and procedure. BS 5750 has extended to other quality assurance systems such as the government initiative 'Investors in People'. I am convinced that all of these movements are part of the general change from 'training for a lifetime of work' to a 'lifetime of training'.

Chapter 8

Internal Verification

 CONCEPTS

An NVQ assessment centre
The job of the internal verifier
Sampling
Quality control of the centre
Moderation of objective tests
Formal examination methods

AN NVQ ASSESSMENT CENTRE

Internal verification systems depend on linking frontline assessors with the accreditation body. Effective control and accuracy in assessment is achieved when the main control is close to primary assessors. The NVQ Centre system is a good example of this technique, so I will continue to use the example for a description of internal verification.

Because there are so many awarding bodies involved in NVQs, internal verification has been standardized and day-to-day control of quality is concentrated in approved NVQ centres.

All awards are controlled locally by a recognized local centre which is run by an internal verifier who must hold a

TDLB Unit D34. This centre acts as a vital link in the quality control system for all NVQs and maintains links with all NVQ assessors who hold TDLB Units D32 and D33. The centre coordinator also links up the line to the occupational lead body, the awarding body and the NCVQ.

There is now a standardized list of requirements for NVQ centres, which is called the 'Common Accord', drawn up by the NCVQ in consultation with the awarding bodies. The local verifier has the responsibility to make sure that the centre keeps up to the mark in each area. The Common Accord states that all NVQ centres must have:

- Management systems – the Centre specifies and maintains an effective system for managing NVQs and there are effective administrative arrangements
- Physical resources – sufficient resources are available to assess candidates for NVQs
- Staff resources – must be sufficient to deliver assessment for NVQs
- Assessment – a system for valid and reliable assessment to national standards is specified and maintained
- Quality Assurance and control – an effective system is essential
- Equal Opportunities and Access – there is a clear commitment. NCVQ has an overriding responsibility to ensure that awarding bodies have adequate arrangements and resources for quality assurance. This means that: systems have to be checked and approved when an NVQ centre is set up; and the assessment and verification processes have to be maintained throughout the period of accreditation.

Competency-based assessment systems have been criticized by traditional educationalists for a variation in standards but the NCVQ seems to be developing a robust national verification process. The focus of control is placed at the NVQ centre and the common accord promotes the adoption of best practice and aims to improve users' understanding of arrangements.

Best practice has been identified on the basis of cost-effectiveness and fitness for purpose; it should adapt to work within existing employment, education and training structures and utilise, wherever relevant, existing information sources to inform quality assurance.

The Common Accord establishes standard terms for the main functions and roles in the assessment and verification systems.

- Assessment carried out by an NVQ Assessor
- Internal Verification carried out by an NVQ Internal Verifier
- External Verification carried out by an NVQ External Verifier
- Approved Centre approved by an awarding body to offer NVQ assessment as agreed in the Common Accord

NCVQ will therefore require awarding bodies to:

- Ensure the availability of sufficient competent assessors and verifiers.

National standards for assessment and verification exist. It is a logical consequence of the NVQ process that assessors and verifiers should establish their competence by holding certificates of unit credit in the relevant units.

Assessors, internal verifiers and external verifiers will all need sufficient background to enable them to judge whether a candidate's performance is meeting the specified standards of occupational competence. The precise background that will be appropriate will vary between sectors and roles. The awarding body should specify clearly the occupational competence or expertise considered necessary to perform each role. It is recommended that the awarding body seeks advice from the appropriate lead body on this issue to ensure that the standards set are correct.

NCVQ monitoring can be summarized as:

NCVQ officers or their representatives undertake post-accreditation monitoring activities such as attending meet-

, visiting awarding bodies and approved centres, speak-
to candidates and others, checking documentation and
seeing assessment taking place.

The awarding body should review external verifier
reports and prepare annual consolidated reports, identify-
ing the strengths and weaknesses of NVQ arrangements,
with particular reference to assessment, verification and
equal opportunities. The consolidated report should be
made available to NCVQ.

THE JOB OF THE INTERNAL VERIFIER

The NVQ internal verifier (IV) has to hold a TDLB Unit
D34 award. I will go through the elements of D34 to
describe what is involved for the NVQ internal verifier
because it gives sound advice for all involved in this work.

D341 Advise and support assessors
The IV must keep up to date with all the awarding body's
documentation; I find the best way is to produce a procedures book for the whole centre. This can use the centre
approval document as a basis and it should contain all
documents connected with the centre including policy
statements such as equal opportunities policy and the
arrangements for disputes and appeals.

The records of the existing assessment team need to be
kept up to date so that they can act as a guide for regular
staff training. The procedures manual is the basis for the
induction of new members.

The IV has to give advice about:

- the use of different types of evidence in assessment
- candidates with special assessment requirements
- consistency in assessment.

As manager of the assessment centre, the IV must run team
moderation meetings, make sure that everyone is up to
date with the latest information and resources, and allocate
candidates to appropriate assessors. With the increase in

higher level NVQs, the allocation of assessors is becoming a serious issue.

D342 Maintain and monitor arrangements for processing assessment information

Record keeping is an important part of the centre leader's work. Some centres use computerized systems and the entering of data can become a security problem. The IV needs a robust system which collects information as soon as a candidate enters the centre and is easy to access as the programme progresses. Because a number of people are involved in each stage – registration, induction, action planning, evidence collection, observation, review, assessment, verification, external verification and certification – it is usually best for the IV to appoint an office manager to collate and enter all data on the candidates' records.

As with all assessment, security and confidentiality are very important. The IV may have a special problem with security in an NVQ centre because many colleagues and associates take NVQ qualifications in centres which are often at the heart of a busy working organization.

D343 Verify assessment practice

It is the responsibility of the IV to recommend candidates for NVQ qualifications to the awarding body. This means that all the evidence has been checked to make sure that it is authentic, reliable, sufficient and consistent. In practice this can only be achieved by working in very close cooperation with the assessment team.

I have found that the best method is to run regular assessment team meetings in which the assessed portfolios of evidence are verified under the supervision of the IV. This is good team training because it allows for discussion of questions of assessment. Other matters, like information from the awarding body, changes in NCVQ regulations and the up-dating of resources can also be discussed. Regular team meetings are a good opportunity for small presentations for staff development in assessment methods and a suitable time for the induction of new team members.

It is helpful if team meetings are treated formally. If an agenda is drawn up, a regular review of the centre can be encouraged. The minutes can be sent to the external verifier and absent team members. In addition, a record of minutes in the centre procedure manual maintains an up-to-date record for the external verifier. I like the external verifier to play an active role in team meetings and the IV might encourage the external verifier to give short presentations on current issues to the team.

SAMPLING

Once the initial assessment has been made, the internal verifier has some difficulty with samples.

Is the internal verifier's sample to assess the quality of the candidate's evidence? If this is the case, a 10 per cent sample can be taken from an alphabetical list of all the candidates submitting portfolios at the centre.

Is the internal verifier to sample the standard of the assessor's marking? The sample will have to be chosen from each assessor's list of candidates. This might be difficult if there is a large variation in the number of candidates with each assessor.

The centre may have several satellites or outside centres which need to be compared. If that is the case, the IV would have a third sampling choice because the standards of outside assessment would be of particular importance to the external verifier.

Whichever sample is chosen, internal verification is always improved if it is shared by the team of assessors. Internal moderation is an excellent way of helping all members of the team to keep up to date and to get direct feedback on the overall standard of assessment. Samples which contain at least one example of the assessor's own candidate give an ideal chance for a direct comparison with other assessor's work. The IV may be asked to collect together a sample for the external moderator, and such a good staff training opportunity should not be missed. When any sample of candidate's work is collected together, the IV should give the assessment team members a chance to inspect the portfolios at the same time.

QUALITY CONTROL OF THE CENTRE

It was sad when the South Thames Training and Enterprise Council folded at the beginning of 1995 because some of its work was excellent. My training and development office took part in a quality control exercise with STTEC only a week before the end of trading. Table 8.1 gives an outline of the criteria and the possible indicators which formed the basis of our centre appraisal. They are simple but turned out to be highly effective.

Table 8.1 *Centre appraisal criteria and indicators*

Criteria	*Possible indicators*
Information	
1. The centre should communicate the services they are offering	1.1 Information covers all major topics of relevance to NVQ candidates, in particular the range of assessment methods available 1.2 Information is – up-to-date – accurate 1.3 Information is free of charge
2. Up-to-date information on NVQ availability and training opportunities are accessible within the centre	2.1 Access to appropriate computer databases – NCVQ database – TAPS/CAPITAL 2.2 Availability of paper records /NVQ updates
Management of centre	
3. The centre has a service that is managed to ensure standards are maintained	3.1 A named person is responsible for managing the service and maintaining quality of service 3.2 A named person is available to deal with day-to-day issues and to take referrals

4. The centre keeps appropriate records and statistical information

4.1 Records and statistical systems meet the awarding body require ments
4.2 Records are regularly updated – indicate frequency of up-dates

5. Systems are in place to monitor the effective-ness of the assessment service offered

5.1 Outcomes of NVQs and units achieved are monitored

Service delivery

6. Assessment is available on demand

6.1 Assessment is not dependent on participation in a learning/ training programme
6.2 Assessment costs are separately calculated
6.3 Unit certification is available on demand

7. An area is available for assessment interviews

7.1 A designated interview area is available which affords privacy, quiet, comfortable furnishings, access to an external telephone

8. The centre delivers a quality assessment service

8.1 Initial enquiries are acknowledged within 48 hours
8.2 Guidance interviews for assessment services are booked within two weeks of initial responses

9. Staff employed in the assessment centre demonstrate competence through being appropriately qualified

9.1 Staff involved in assessment are vocationally competent as laid down by the awarding body
9.2 Assessors, verifiers and APL advisers have appropriate TDLB units
9.3 Staff who provide information only are trained to do so, have full knowledge of the information system and follow established procedures

9.4 Records of staff development
activities relating to assessor
and adviser awards

10. Individuals receive
sufficient pre-entry
information to enable
informed choices to be
made

10.1 Client entitlement statement
to NVQ services is made available
10.2 Details of pricing structure
are clear and readily available

11. Individuals are
considered for NVQ
assessment and/or
training as
appropriate

11.1 Individuals are screened to
establish suitability for the
recommended learning/assessment
route

12. APL service is
available, appropriate
to individual needs

12.1 APL advisers are qualified
with Unit D36
12.2 APL opportunities are identified
on entry
12.3, Assistance is given with
APL portfolio building

13. Action plans and
assessment plans show
evidence of realistic
guidance and a full
range of assessment
opportunities

13.1 Assessment plans make maximum
use of naturally occurring evidence
in the workplace
13.2 APL is integrated where
appropriate
13.3 All documentation given to
clients is legible and uses
appropriate language which is free
from jargon
13.4 Action plans reflect individual
circumstances and
preferences

14. Individuals are kept
informed of their
achievements and future
opportunities following
assessment

14.1 Records of guidance and
advice to individuals at the
conclusion of their development/
assessment programme

━━━━━━━━━━━━━ **ACTIVITY** ━━━━━━━━━━━━━

Checking your own centre.
If you are associated with an NVQ centre or if you are thinking about setting one up, check through this list of criteria and possible indicators to see how well your centre fits the requirements.

MODERATION OF OBJECTIVE TESTS

In objective tests the assessment and internal moderation take place before the test is carried out. It may not be the centre team which writes the objective items but they have to be written by people at that level, and established item banks have to be constantly updated with material from people at the marker and assessor level. Some of the worst books of objective item examples are written by publishing editorial teams who are out of touch with both the subject matter and the current examples. I worked with the Metropolitan Police at Hendon in London when they were developing objective item tests for promotion examinations within the service. To give the examiner team current practical examples, each year four newly qualified police constables were recruited as an item writing team, an excellent way of keeping up to date.

One judgement which has to be made in objective item testing is the policy on guessing. I encourage my students to put in an answer in all objective item testing because it is impossible for an assessor to judge what is an informed guess but a mistake, and what is blind chance. Because it is impossible to decide between error and uninformed gambling most marking systems have abandoned any correction for wrong responses so the candidate might just as well fill in one of the choices. Random selection gives everyone a chance of gaining 25 per cent in any objective item test even if they are ignorant of the subject. Computer marking can pick up a candidate who tries to beat the system by filling in more than one response box but it cannot identify why the choice was made.

Item statistics can be stored in computers so that the level of objective item tests can be closely controlled. Here are three statistics usually measured for each item:

- subject area
- the effectiveness of 'distracters' – alternatives which are not the correct answer or key
- difficulty, in the form of how many candidates who succeed in the test as a whole in getting the particular item right.

Internal moderation and quality control in item bank testing are based on the formation of the overall test specification and the detailed statistics for each item on the bank.

FORMAL EXAMINATION METHODS

There are two systems which can be used for internal moderation of examination marking. A subject matter specialist can be appointed internal moderator for a section of an examination, or the whole of an examination if there is a small number of candidates; this internal moderator has the following duties:

- to agree a marking plan for each question with the team of markers assigned to the question. This can be carried out before the examination and, if the team are new to the job, the marking team can be briefed at the same time
- once a marker starts on a question, the internal moderator checks every tenth answer. This re-marking has to be done quickly at the beginning because if the internal moderator is not satisfied with the standard of marking, the moderator may have to give further instructions about the required standard and the marker will be asked to start again.

The second method of internal moderation which can be used in an examination is the resolution of marks after 'blind double marking'. The method works in this way:

- The first marker is given the examination paper, a pile of answers to one of the questions and a form which has the name of the examination, the number of the question, the first marker's name and a list of the candidate examination numbers which corresponds to the answers in the pile.
- The first marker does not write comments on the scripts but makes notes and puts a mark on the form opposite the candidate's examination number.
- The examinations officer keeps the form containing the first marker's comments and marks and issues the same pile of answers with an examination paper and a new form with the second marker's name at the top and the same list of candidate numbers.
- When all the marking has been carried out a meeting is called for the resolution of marks. Sometimes the differences between markers are easy to resolve but the scripts are available in case there is difficulty in coming to a conclusion. Resolved marks are recorded by the examinations officer. I used to enjoy resolution meetings but the method is time-consuming because every script is seen twice.

Both methods are excellent for inducting new members of staff to marking standards and both help to maintain an even standard of marking across all scripts.

================================ **ACTIVITY** ================================

Moderating a written test.
You may not use full examination marking but the principles for moderation can be applied to even simple written tests. If you use written tests regularly, work out a system of double marking or internal moderation.

Chapter 9

Trends in Assessment

 CONCEPTS

New pathways
Computer assessment
The trend to peer and self-assessment
Assessment affecting funding

NEW PATHWAYS

A recent article on pathways (*Competence and Assessment*, June 1995) produced by the Engineering Council, put forward a series of plans for a more flexible approach to registration within the profession. The basic entry level covered:

A levels
GNVQ National Diploma
Modern apprenticeship (which bridged full-time and part-time study)
NVQ levels 2 and 3
BTEC First and National
Work-based learning

This is the range of possible starting places for learners who wish to enter engineering as a career; it also represents a number of different methods and philosophies of assessment. There is a trend towards linking very different routes to higher education. The training/education divide seems to be disappearing under economic pressure for a highly skilled workforce which is literate, numerate and able to communicate.

With higher level NVQs in higher education the two separate assessment systems have to be merged. My own office has established the links between NVQ units and units within the Certificate in Education, BA degree and MA. At present the situation is very flexible. Some extracts about the relationship between NVQs and higher education presented by Otter (1994) are shown in Table 9.1

Table 9.1 *Relationship between NVQs and higher education*

Academic/theoretical degree programmes

Nature of the course/ relevance to NVQs	Academic knowledge: of limited or no relevance to NVQs
Assessment implications	None
Relationship with NVQs	None
Requirement for certification through NVQ awarding body	No

Applied degree programme

Nature of the course/ relevance to NVQs	Curriculum could be informed by NVQ standards in some areas Possibility of NVQ units on work placements Implications for GNVQs
Assessment implications	There is assessment of competence but not to NVQ

	standards Assessment in the workplace would need to be to NVQ standards
Relationship with NVQs	Dual accreditation, or additional certification at place of work
Requirement for certification through NVQ awarding body	Yes in some areas

Degrees leading to professional qualifications

Nature of the course/ *relevance to NVQs*	Curriculum related to NVQ units in some areas, especially in underpinning knowledge Work placement may lead to NVQ units at level 4 and 5
Assessment implications	Assessment of relevant NVQs
Relationship with NVQs	Dual accreditation
Requirement for certification through NVQ awarding body	Yes in some areas

Continuing professional development

Nature of the course/ *relevance to NVQs*	Curriculum provides and assesses knowledge component of NVQ Level 5 Work practice assessed at work by professionals HE responsible for developing reflective practice and professional capacity

Assessment implications	Assessment to NVQ standards
Relationship with NVQs	NVQ certification or dual accreditation
Requirement for certification through NVQ awarding body	Yes

⇨   **STOP AND REFLECT**   ⇦

What are the pathways for training in your own area?

Do the academic and competence routes join together? If so could you tell a learner how to bridge these different methods of assessment?

How would a practioner follow continuous professional development in your area?

COMPUTER ASSESSMENT

I have been interested in computer assessment ever since I was introduced to a fiendish card system on the Atlas computer of the University of London. Until recently this has been a peripheral interest but now that event-driven computer training is with us, effective assessment and report writing by computer is a realistic option for assessment.

Authoring programs for developing computer training vary but they all contain some features in common (Asymetrix, 1995). There are two ways in which the program can be read: author and user. Both see the material on the screen and interaction can take place with what is displayed, but the user has limited access and can only add responses to questions and instructions. The author can alter instructions and functions as part of the instruction-building process. Sound, still pictures and video clips can now be added to an interactive (event-driven) program.

Computer learning and simulation seem to be the doorway to a new era of instruction and training.

An author of computer training programs can build assessment into the learning system. Individual responses to questioning can be summarized as self-assessment feedback which encourages progress. A cumulative summary of progress through a series of computer lessons can be made. These assessments can be matched to course or program requirements so that students can have a computer summary of their learning achievement. It is possible for the trainer or teacher to write into the program a reporting system so that a written report can be produced at the end of a training session.

Part of my reaction to these developments is to be horrified by the mechanistic approach but there is a great deal to be gained from colour, sound, action, beautiful pictures, curiosity and endless worldwide information in computer learning. The computer seems to open the door to effective learning and hopefully the associated assessment can be equally imaginative.

⇨   **STOP AND REFLECT**   ⇦

How would you exploit the use of computer learning and assessment in your own area?

Do you think that learners would feel cheated and resentful if their assessment came out of a computer terminal?

THE TREND TO PEER AND SELF-ASSESSMENT

Learning how to assess your peers is invaluable in the process of learning interpersonal skills. Effective self-assessment is essential in reflective learning. Unfortunately these methods of assessment have two serious drawbacks: there is a tendency to record subjective feelings and personality traits rather than objective reports; and they are cheap. All other methods of assessment are expensive, sometimes very expensive, and so training managers tend to choose peer and self-assessment even when they are inappropriate.

I shudder when I think of peer assessment after a ghastly three days at our staff college near Bristol. The programme for women managers was run by an enthusiastic woman who made a group of normally sensible women carry out a series of exercises which they hated. How she managed to beguile us all I have no idea but the ultimate final peer assessment was typical. We were forced to strap a large blank sheet of paper onto our backs. We were provided with felt pens and were asked to write, anonymously, what we thought of another person on her back. Our pent-up irritation caused some fairly nasty words to fly but none more so than on the back of that dreadful woman. It is difficult to express the trepidation which I felt when I took the paper off my back and read what others had said about me. In the event I had an easy time because the only thing that anyone said was: 'She is brave!'

Personality traits and subjective feelings are not difficult to predict. In America, where every type of human assessment and testing continues to be popular in training and management, the psychologists have made quite a business of teaching employees to achieve positive reports. An American friend, who taught psychology, once told me how he coached his colleagues into getting good reports from students. At that time no staff in his college could obtain permanent posts unless they achieved regular good class reports. The technique was to play on the basic insecurity of students at the beginning of a semester and then to build dependence on the teacher, by intermittent rewards, so that the students were convinced that they could only achieve success with the help of the class teacher. Unfortunately this type of manipulation is very effective and can be learned.

There are some areas where peer and self-assessment are widely used, such as the caring professions, and they go well with strong mentorship systems of training. There have been many attempts to introduce objectivity into the assessment methods and some techniques are now so easy to use that personal feelings rarely creep in.

Using a checklist

Well-prepared checklists, which are based on job analysis, encourage balanced and uniform reporting. I read through the BA marking rating scale each time before marking an assignment; it feels rather like checking the required tasks to service a car. Checklists are useful for peer or self-assessment because they keep the observations firmly fixed on the essentials.

Questionnaires and rating scales

These can be useful tools, but they are prone to be influenced by the person who devises them. One of the principal arguments against direct democratic rule is 'Who gets to write the questions?' I remember the debate about Britain's entry into Europe, when most people voted for entry and only a few with strong political views voted against. Can I be sure that this reflected true public opinion or was the question drafted to achieve a particular result?

⇨ STOP AND REFLECT ⇦

When you read a questionnaire, can you detect any bias behind the questions?

If you feel that you cannot answer 'Yes' or 'No' to a question, can you write a better question which everyone finds relevant?

Do you feel that some questions only cover half of what you want to say on an issue? If so, how should the question be improved?

The trouble with most questionnaires is that they represent what the questioner wants answered and not what the answerer wants to say.

Every questionnaire has the aim of gathering factual evidence or testing a hypothesis, it is a great mistake to confuse the two. If you want to test a hypothesis, choose a research method and plan your research using questionnaires as a method of gathering information. What you must *not* do is rush out with a questionnaire, collect a few facts and then make decisions on the basis of unreliable material. Unless a questionnaire is part of an overall data collection procedure the information is of very little use.

These are the steps which must be followed when preparing a questionnaire:

- turn to page 60 and re-read the section on attitude testing and rating scales before writing your questionnaire
- make two lists of questions: one designed to gather the facts you require and the other to test opinions
- check your questions with a colleague before trying the questions on a small group of respondents
- make certain to record what these trial respondents would have liked to have been asked as well as the general impression of your questions
- edit your draft with two colleagues, if possible, and then take care in the layout and presentation of the questionnaire
- validate your questionnaire with a random sample taken from the group you want to test
- collate the results into a form which can be used for evaluation and retest the questionnaire once the evaluators have decided if the information gathered is useful.

ACTIVITY

Peer assessment at work.
It is not always necessary to write the qualities on a rating scale. Here is rather a neat method of peer assessment which you may like to try out at work.
Ask a colleague to complete the following questionnaire about your performance at work:

Write down the five most important characteristics or personal qualities which are required in this field of work and rate my performance on the scale provided.

Qualities	Excellent	Good	Average	Weak	Poor
1. Knowledge of training and assessment		✓			
2. Empathy with learners	✓				
3. etc					
4.					
5.					

Personal reports

The report writer has to strive to be objective and avoid letting personal feelings creep in. Sometimes critics do not even bother to conceal personal feelings. I once asked for an opinion about a book which I was thinking of recommending to the students. Subsequently the book became highly influential in education and far beyond. The short report said: 'Thank you for the book – I enjoyed scanning it! In parts the indulgent and whimsical use of language grated – and certainly caused this reader to reject the content. I also believe that such books are used by some able students to increase their manipulative skills rather than more positive interpersonal skills. But thanks anyway!'

Several techniques can be adopted to make personal reports more objective.

Being positive first

This is a sound recommendation for all critics but you do have to be sincere. My mother told a story about a scrupulously honest woman who hovered for a very long time over a pram containing a remarkably ugly baby; as she stood up she murmured with great sincerity, 'Doesn't he look comfortable!'

Reports should be open

One of the main criteria in the NVQ assessor awards is that feedback should be as immediate as possible and that all reports about another person's performance should be open. If you are not prepared to read the report aloud and face-to-face with the people involved then it is possible that your report contains personal bias which you are not prepared to defend.

Check the status of the reporter

Make sure that the expert is still qualified to give a worthwhile opinion. So many fields of expertise change quickly these days and some people fail to keep up to date with professional development and yet claim to be something of an authority. One of the advantages of NVQ qualifications is that 'old hands' have to prove that they still have current expertise.

ASSESSMENT AFFECTING FUNDING

In both training and education there seems to be a trend towards more assessment of institutions and organizations so that decisions about funding can be made. All funding depends directly or indirectly on customer satisfaction. Since our jobs depend on it, we must pay careful attention to the way in which our work is assessed and valued by the funding authorities. The systems which collect and evaluate assessments of work in training and education are complex but they are usually available to trainers and teachers, so it is important to keep up to date in your field. Here is a case study of the current situation in technical and vocational education in the UK.

Recently there have been some basic changes in the funding of technical colleges and sixth-form colleges and the funding policy of the Further Education Funding Council (FEFC) is still undergoing change so I can use this volatile sector as an example.

The FEFC has a budget of £31 billion pounds for 463 FE colleges in England. There are about 100 sixth-form colleges which are included in this group. The FEFC is moving away from the concept of full-time student equivalent but at present the gross unit cost related to the full time equivalent (FTE) for one year's cost ranges from £1,400, an average of £2,600, to a maximum of £3,600. This was not a comparison of like with like because some programmes such as agriculture and engineering are expensive whereas 'talk and chalk' programmes are cheaper. Staff: student ratio, class size and student contact hours have changed, but in FE they were running at a staff student ratio of 13 or 14 to 1 in 1992. Average class sizes have risen slightly to 16. There has also been a slight increase in lecturers' teaching hours to 18.2 hours per week but it is the number of hours that a student has in class contact that has seen the biggest change. Student contact with lecturers has been reduced to 22.3 hours per week; in some areas like engineering the number of hours contact has been reduced to 19.5 hours per week.

The FEFC has laid down some ground rules for the new funding which include the following.

The Unit

This is a basic funding unit called the 'Unit of activity'. It is to become the currency in which a college can work with weighting for different programmes and types of student. The unit can be used to give overall departmental figures for the activities going on and the funding from the FEFC can be calculated in terms of the overall unit count for an FE college.

Simplicity

The FEFC aims at a simple system but this is hard to achieve given the complexity of the situation.

Movement away from FTE

The concept of the full time student is due to be phased out because of the emphasis on 'time served' rather than the learning achieved. It is hoped that the bench mark of FTE is replaced by an aim at a '100 unit' student.

The 100 unit student

Units will be divided into three stages for a single student: entry, on programme, and the achievement phase. This is one of the strengths of the new system in that a college can gain units for active advertising and the induction of students. A maximum of eight units (in the nominal 100) are awarded for this entry phase of the student point score and some APL is covered in the area. The bulk of the units are attracted in the 'on programme' phase which is defined by the student being 'with a member of staff'; on the programme there is a complex tariff advisory system with the following features:

- *Individually listed qualifications* which are a guide to the number of units which can be claimed per student per qualification, eg, BTEC Higher National Certificate: 65.5, BTEC National Diploma: 168.0.
- *Other qualifications.* Programmes which are not individually listed fit into a load band system which depends on the number of hours/year that a student is expected to study for a particular programme. This ranges from 3.8 units for band 1 with a student on a qualification occupying 9 – 59 hours/year, to 84 units for band 6 with at least 450 hours per year. Distance learning students are usually counted on load band 3.
- *More than one qualification.* Scores for two or more qualifications are added together so that an additional A level will add 18.4 to the score.
- *Cost weighting factor.* To counteract the difference in costs – say between engineering and an arts subject and because of the smaller numbers in practical workshop classes – there is a weighting list which is given in a *very* long list of qualifications.
- *Points gained by students themselves.* Individual students can gain extra points if they fall into one of the following categories:
    - any full-time, unwaged 16 – 19-year-student
    - anyone on full national security benefit

- any dependant (unwaged) of someone on full
 benefit
- anyone who requires primary education or
 English Support in 16 – 19 age group
- anyone who requires learner support.

The achievement units can be claimed at any time but there are no units awarded if the student leaves the college. The cut-off dates are 1 November, 1 February, and 15 May, which makes the problem of retention critical for the colleges.

Quality Control

The FEFC runs an inspection system where colleges are rated on a 1, excellent, to 5, poor, scale. It is interesting to note that when colleges are compared with average 1 to 5 inspection scale rating ie, a comparison between overall cost and overall quality, there is no correlation between cost and quality.

This system of bringing the FE colleges gradually into a universal funding system has the aim of boosting recruitment, retention, and results. Before leaving the topic of funding, here is a personal note on your taxation allowances. Individuals who are in employment and paying standard rate income tax can claim tax rebate on all NVQ training qualifications. The same tax concessions apply to this series of books because you cannot study training without the understanding of learning and assessment. If you bought this book, or any in this series, you can claim tax allowance on your next tax form!

Chapter 10

Self-evaluation and Appraisal

 CONCEPTS

Autonomy
Self-checks on your performance
Observing your learners' reactions
Appraisal
An example of appraisal

AUTONOMY

The purpose of education, training, human resource development, continuous professional development, investment in people, becoming a learning opportunist or whatever title is given to learning after the age of 16, is to achieve the ability to act independently: 'autonomy'. This series has encouraged the reader to master how people learn, how to understand their own learning preferences, how to tackle their own barriers to learning and strategies for independent learning. Now you must be able to evaluate yourself so that you can help others to evaluate themselves.

SELF-CHECKS ON YOUR PERFORMANCE

Many self-checks have been devised for teachers and trainers on performance but they are all based on some general rules and these can be summed up as

What are you trying to do?
Setting a good example.
Teaching activities.
Professional pride in teaching and training.

What are you trying to do?

Before you can assess the quality of your own performance you need to clarify the aim of your activity. Paul Hirst (1970) laid down three necessary conditions for teaching which apply equally well to training. These are:

- the intention to bring about learning – the student must learn something. To find out how effective you have been there will have to be some form of pre-test for the learner to find out where he or she starts from and then, after you have done your worst, a test to find out what has been learnt
- the clarification of what has to be learnt – the student must know what is to be learnt. Teaching and training are not processes of indoctrination and the learner must be a willing participant in the activity so that you must be able to demonstrate how you introduced the learning topics
- the achievement of learning aims – teaching is the art of the possible and the student must, given every foreseeable factor, be able to achieve the learning aims and desired competencies.

⇨ **STOP AND REFLECT** ⇦

What do you intend your learners to learn?
What has to be achieved before your learners start?

> Have you selected students who will benefit from the learning experience?
>
> It can be very damaging for learners to fail and, if they started at the beginning because you gave unrealistic advice, your encouragement might be self-indulgence.

Setting a good example

When one of my infant sons called me 'Bloody Mummy', I realized, with some shame, that I must clean up my language and I worried about my language in front of the classes at my technical college. Effective trainers and teachers are role models for their learners whatever the age of the students. Remember that you may be setting the standards and working practice of a lifetime for other people. You may be a front-line representative of a trade or profession and you certainly are a representative of teachers and trainers. Here are some areas in which it is most important for you to set a good example.

Health and safety at work

This is the most important area in which a correct example must be set at all times. Safe working practice is so difficult to teach and clear exemplars are by far the best. You should be a model of the latest and correct working practice; a correct follower of all health and safety rules and procedures; and wear safety clothing, footwear and personal protection equipment whenever necessary.

I am sure that there is a learning bonus if you not only wear the right things and carry out the right procedures but you look stylish in your protective helmet and make correct procedure visibly the most efficient method to adopt.

Showing a positive attitude

When the teacher or trainer presents learning in a trade, profession or industry as a boring process, with little interest; and as an unfortunate necessity which has to be endured to earn some money, the learner is being prepared for a lifetime of dull routine at the best and deep-seated personal dissatisfaction at the worst. Why should the student bother to learn? Why does the teacher or trainer bother to stay in such an unsatisfactory role? Depression, cynicism and open hostility to the system and to the management are rotten motivators. Too many long-serving teachers and trainers seem to adopt these postures. I think that such behaviour is a clear indication of internal conflict and poor intrapersonal skills. For good motivation you need to show pride in your work, an enthusiasm for the subject, and positive attitudes to future developments.

On the other hand, such positive approaches to work must be based on sensible consideration of all of the facts and the teacher and trainer must 'engage brain' when being positive. Nothing is easier to destroy by negative criticism than silly, senseless overenthusiasm.

$\Rightarrow$ **STOP AND REFLECT** $\Leftarrow$

Do you sneer at the young and enthusiastic?
Do you take a pride in your work?

Showing empathy for your learners

One trainer I know is hooked on the motto, 'Manners maketh man'. It is surprising how a phrase which can be seen as a sexist remark by one person can illuminate a shining truth to another. This trainer is not alone: 'Manners maketh man' was the motto chosen by William of Wykeham, the founder of the first English school, Winchester College, and when the Lord Bishop chose the word 'manners' he meant the whole of education, but I understand what my colleague means. He is regretting the passing of old-fashioned courtesy and good manners in present-day society. When I stand strap-hanging in a crowded London tube with healthy young brutes lounging in the seats before me, I too regret that grandmothers are no longer given seats; but my friend is making a more serious point. Courteous behaviour to everyone is the enemy of discrimination, prejudice and poor social skills. If you make sure that every learner is treated with consideration and politeness then most interpersonal difficulties melt away. In your self-assessment, ask yourself whether you:

have positive expectations of your learners
recognize individuality
pay equal attention to each learner's contribution
encourage those who are diffident and shy.

Teaching activities

You can be observed by another person but you yourself may be the best judge of your own activities because you know more clearly than anyone else what you want to achieve.

ACTIVITY

Immediate check on your learning session.
There are lots of activities you can use to encourage learning. Run through this list to see how many common ways you have just used to help learning. Did you try . . .

Analysing	Applying	Breaking down
Characterizing	Classifying	Comparing
Contrasting	Describing	Distinguishing
Enumerating	Explaining	Giving examples
Illustrating	Imagining	Making word pictures
Pointing out	Proving	Questioning
Reminding	Specifying	Spelling out
Structuring	Summarizing	Wondering

Professional pride in teaching and training

A long time ago I decided that there was no kind 'headmaster in the sky' who would tell me what a good girl I was if I took care in my teaching preparation and pride in my work. Like housework, where no one ever says 'Thank you' for good cleaning work, the committed teacher and trainer has to rely on self-regulation as a measure of professional skill. Promotion and monetary rewards in teaching and training seem to be given for every other job but successfully helping the learner to learn! Nowadays I take pride in my teaching performance for my own satisfaction and to my own exacting standard and I recommend that you do the same. Once you have decided that self-regulation is important to your own self-image you may find yourself to be a hard taskmaster but you will take pride in being:

punctual
careful in preparation
honest and accurate in feedback and record keeping
the producer of inspiring learning sessions.

OBSERVING YOUR LEARNERS' REACTIONS

Teaching and training are catalytic work. It is sometimes sensible to remind ourselves that, given enough time, the learner could have achieved the learning anyway. It is our job to speed the rate of learning just as a catalyst accelerates the rate of reaction. At the end of our efforts, the learner moves on and we have to start again with another novice group. This natural cycle of teaching and learning means that the attitude of the learner to the teacher changes. At first the learner is highly dependent on the tutor's guidance, but as the learner begins to gain confidence and competence his or her view of the teacher changes. I have always resisted the temptation to play back early videos of my student's performance at the end of the programme because I regard that as unkind, but I have never been surprised that I get glowing and excellent feedback reports at the beginning of a programme and some kind but often patronizing ones when I have launched my students well.

Anonymous written reports from students may have a limited use but there are plenty of ways in which you can get feedback from the learners. In some biological experiments the researcher looks for 'indicators', like testing the purity of river water by the presence of indicator plants and insects. What we have to do in this activity is find out which indicators mean that you are really helping the learner to progress. You will have to work out the best indicators for your own situation but here are some suggestions.

'Voting with their feet'

I have always found that attendance is a crude but robust measure of how well I am doing. Ask yourself if your learners turn up for meetings, classes, works visits, or out-of-hours activities. Do they come on time or do they slide in late with poor excuses? I used to encourage prompt attendance by giving clear hints about the next assignment in the first five minutes of class and refusing to repeat what I had said when the latecomers arrived. Many teachers strive hard to help latecomers to catch up with what has gone on before their arrival. I have always thought that this effort hard on those who had taken the trouble to arrive on time. I try to make latecomers wait until I have progressed the whole class to some activity during which I can help the latecomer to catch up. Work out your own measure for attendance and punctuality among your learners but do not be bullied by a few to disadvantage the whole group.

Identification

A sure indicator that you are doing well in a group is when individuals start to identify with your learning sessions. 'We are going to do . . .', 'What will we be doing next . . . ?' are clear indications that the learners are beginning to identify with your teaching. I hate it when learners drop out from my groups, especially evening classes or unpopular programmes on to which the learners have been conscripted rather than volunteered. It is a measure of my success when such groups stick together or even grow with deserters from other classes. This expansion can make a teacher or trainer very unpopular with colleagues, so if you are working in a team you should try to make the identification apply to the whole group – rather more of the 'us' than 'we'.

Individual learner's identification with good teaching and training comes in the form of recommendations. I suspect that many join programmes and courses because of word-of-mouth and popular images. 'When you go to Garnett try to get Len Powell as a tutor' was what I was told long ago. Look out for examples of new students wanting to join your groups.

Enjoyment

There have been times in my teaching career when I have had so much fun with the class that I really look forward to the next session and I am sad when the programme comes to an end. For some reason, unhelpful surroundings and unprepossessing students make the enjoyment greater: the achievement of less likely success makes the victory sweeter. Any fool can help bright students to successful learning but the slow dawning of understanding or the final achievement of a task which is difficult to master can make the teacher wonder about being paid to do such a satisfying job! Look out for signs that your learners are enjoying themselves as well.

Success

Successful students are a measure of your effectiveness and should be taken as an indicator of your teaching, but as explained on page 27, this must be a measure of value added and not a shrewd selection of who should be entered.

━━━━━━━━━━ **ACTIVITY** ━━━━━━━━━━

What do your learners think about your performance?
Here is an activity to find out if you have 'hooked your learners'. Work out your own indicators of:

'Voting with their feet'
Identification
Enjoyment
Success.

APPRAISAL

Appraisal affords an excellent opportunity for each individual to carry out a complete self-evaluation each year. As an employee approaching retirement, I use my appraisal each year to check progress and refine my own personal plan. Some years ago I wrote myself an action plan because I felt that few managers paid attention to the end of a career; I did not want to shuffle away from the work and professional contacts which had been so absorbing for so many years. I recommend that all teachers and trainers at whatever stage in their career produce their own personal plan. When you make your short-term and long-term plans explicit and you have a clear idea of where you want to go then all other assessment, evaluation and indeed, appraisal, becomes a positive help to your own plan and not an uncomfortable intrusion from outside. No doubt your bosses will be glad to know that they are being useful!

In 1992 teachers in further education colleges in England and Wales joined many others in education and commercial training in being required to have an annual appraisal. Appraisal can be an emotive word and cause anxiety, but I have placed appraisal firmly in this chapter on self-evaluation because I am convinced that it is of great benefit to the teacher or trainer. After years of working with no inspection I enjoyed going through my paces with my first HMI (Her Majesty's Inspector). My chap said that he would sit at the back of my class and take no part while he made his observation. I was delighted when suddenly he was on his feet taking a vocal part in a lively student activity after only 20 minutes in class. I had to call him to order with all the rest; it is nice to know that even HMIs are human. My first appraisals have been very useful too.

Here is a checklist of good practice for appraisal. It comes from the details of an appraisal scheme at a good technical college but the principles apply to all appraisal whether in the state or private sector, commercial, professional or industrial.

CHECKLIST FOR APPRAISAL

1. The scheme must be consistent with the college's mission statement, quality policy and policy aims.
2. Appraisal should form a central part of the college's staff development policy and be interlinked with that policy and with strategies for its delivery.
3. Individual appraisal should be clearly linked to course team, sectional and college reviews, providing a two-way formative process.
4. The principal aim of the appraisal scheme should be:

- to enhance the quality of the service provided by the college for students, employers and the community through the professional and personal development of its staff.

Subsidiary aims are:

- continual improvement in the quality of teaching and learning
- the facilitation of change and curriculum innovation with appropriate support for staff
- institutional development.

5. Guiding principles:the scheme should

- be constructive and non-judgemental

- preserve confidentiality
- encourage the recognition and sharing of good practice
- be separate from other procedures, eg, on discipline, promotion and pay

6. The scheme should be based on a two-year cycle and allow for appraisal of all full-time staff, all staff on fractional contracts and, where possible, part-time staff.

7. The procedures for appraisal should provide for:

- a preparatory meeting between appraiser and appraised to explore and agree parameters for the process; such parameters may include agreement on the range of data to be used, eg, data on the whole of an employee's duties including management tasks and, if appropriate, observation of teaching
- review of previous appraisals
- self-appraisal, including reflection on experience and issues
- a review interview between appraiser and appraised
- an agreed written record of the outcome, including an action plan which can be shared with the appropriate line manager
- mechanisms for dealing with the outcome
- appropriate documentation.

There should be some choice of appraiser, both to promote equality of opportunity(eg, in terms of gender and race) and to allow for personal differences. Consideration should be given to using both line and functional managers and peers (chosen from specially trained cross-college personnel). Consideration will also be given to involving different staff in aspects of appraisal, eg, observation of teaching.

9. No appraiser should normally undertake more than eight appraisals per annum.

10. All staff should receive training to ensure they are familiar with the appraisal process and all appraisers with appropriate techniques. Special arrangements should be made for the training of new staff.

11. There should be an appraisal committee whose task will be to monitor and evaluate the workings of the scheme and ensure its continued linkage to institutional development.
12. There should be an established complaints procedure to deal with any disputes or grievances arising from the appraisal.

AN EXAMPLE OF APPRAISAL

Here is a summary of the appraiser's preparation form for lecturing staff at the University of Greenwich. It is standard of its type and should give you a clear idea of what to expect in the appraisal interview.

This form should help you:

- Look back at your performance over the past year.
- Look forward to the year ahead and the main tasks you see yourself undertaking.
- Look at your personal training and development needs.

1. List your key activities and responsibilities during the past year

2. *Your performance over the past year*
Using your copy of the last appraisal report form (where one exists) please comment upon the results you have achieved against each agreed objective and your standard of performance. If this is your first appraisal, attempt to identify your key job objectives, your expected standards of performance and how well you have achieved them.

What were your most significant achievements during the past year?

Were there any lost opportunities during the year? If so, what were they and why?

Have any objectives needed to be changed or added to? How and why?

Did parts of your job cause you particular difficulty? Why?

Were there constraints on the effectiveness of your performance? What were they?

Comment on the level of support and appropriateness of the management/supervisory style of those you perceive to be your manager(s).

How far was last year's agreed action plan achieved?

What factors, if any, thwarted its full achievement?

In what ways has any recent staff development/training increased the effectiveness of your performance?

3. *The year ahead*
Bearing in mind what you know of the strategies and plans for the university and faculty/school/department, identify your preferred objectives for the year ahead. If there are significant changes from last year please indicate the reasons. Do you perceive any significant constraints on your performance?

4. *Training and development needs*
What training/professional development would contribute to your effectiveness in the year ahead?
What training/professional development needs do you have over the next three years?

ACTIVITY

Write your own appraisal form as self-evaluation.
What better way to finish this book than to fill in this form for yourself to start your own system of self-evaluation!

References

Asymetrix (1995) Multimedia ToolBook, CBT Edition, 3DFIX, InfoModeler, VroomBooks Compact disc.

Bloom, Benjamin S (1964) *The Taxonomy of Educational Objectives*, London: Longman.

Competence and Assessment (1995) 'Pathways', 29, June, The Engineering Council, London

Cronbach, LJ (1984) *Essentials of Psychological Testing*, 4th edition, New York: Harper Row.

Fransella F and Bannister D, (1977) *A Manual for Repertory Grid Technique*, London: Academic Press.

Gardner, Howard (1985) *The Mind's New Science*, New York: Basic Books.

Hebb, DO (1949) *The Organization of Behaviour: A neuropsychological theory*, New York: Wiley.

Hirst, PH and Peters RS, (1970) *The Logic of Education*, London: Routledge and Kegan Paul.

Howell, David C (1982) *Statistical Methods for Psychology*, Duxbury Press, Boston, MA: PWS Publishers.

Kelly, GA (1955) *The Psychology of Personal Constructs*, vol 1 and 2, New York: Norton.

Likert, Rensis (1932) 'A technique for the measurement of attitudes', *Archives of Psychology*, 140, 52.

Otter, S (1994) 'Higher level NVQs/SVQs' conference at Nottingham Trent University.

Popham, W James (1978) Criterion-referenced Measurement, Englewood Cliffs, NJ: Prentice-Hall.

Rowntree, Derek (1989) *Assessing Students: How shall we know them?* revised edition, London: Kogan Page.

Ryle, Gilbert (1949) *The Concept of Mind*, Harmondsworth: Penguin Books.

Super and Crites (1962) *Appraising Vocational Fitness by Means of Psychological Tests*, New York: Harper and Brothers.

Thurstone, Louis, (1929) *The Measurement of Attitudes*, University of Chicago Press.

Toplis, J, Dulewicz, V and Fletcher, C (1987) *Psychological Testing*, London: Institute of Personnel Management.

Index